Waynesburg College Library
Waynesburg, Pa. 15370

W9-CLC-321

WITHDRAWN

720.924   M632c

Carter, Peter
AUTHOR

Mies Van der ,Rohe at work
TITLE

720.924   M632c
Carter, Peter
Mies Van der Rohe at work
106949

MAR 15 '78
FEB 23 '78

Mies van der Rohe at Work

Mies van der Rohe at Work

Peter Carter

PRAEGER PUBLISHERS New York · Washington

Mies van der Rohe always derived great pleasure from the informal discussions he had with students and young architects. On these occasions he would invariably make a point of encouraging questions of a general nature because he believed that such questions could probe deep into the essence of things and so be of great significance to architectural development. He was, in fact, convinced that each generation makes its contribution to that development according to how seriously it asks and how clearly it answers these questions.

In this book I have sought to correlate Mies van der Rohe's ideas on architecture—as he expressed them in these discussions—with the methodology of his way of work, in the hope that this information may be found stimulating to a new generation of architects, as well as to the interested layman.

Peter Carter
Chicago 1972

BOOKS THAT MATTER

Praeger Publishers, Inc.
111 Fourth Avenue, New York, N.Y. 10003, U.S.A.

Published in the United States of America in 1974
by Praeger Publishers, Inc.

© 1974 by the Pall Mall Press, London, England
All rights reserved

No part of this publication may be reproduced, stored in a retrieval system, or transmitted in any form or by any means, electronic, mechanical, photocopying, recording, or otherwise, without the prior permission of the copyright owner.

Library of Congress Cataloging in Publication Data

Carter, Peter.
  Mies van der Rohe at work.

  Bibliography: p.
  1. Mies van der Rohe, Ludwig, 1886–1969.
  I. Title.
NA1088.M65037   720'.92'4   72-88260

Printed in Great Britain

Contents

106949

Introduction

The work of one of modern architecture's founding fathers cannot be adequately covered in a single volume, but one may, as is my intention in this book, endeavour to clarify the basic tenets from which the work as a whole unfolds. For Mies van der Rohe, these tenets arose from the interaction of two premises: first, that architecture is derived from, and eventually becomes an expression of the ethos of a civilization; second, that its physical realization is accomplished through the use of clear construction.

ARCHITECTURE AND CIVILIZATION: Mies van der Rohe believed that architecture at its most valuable can be nothing more than a reflection of the driving and sustaining forces of an epoch. It is not a fashion, nor is it something for eternity; it is a part of an epoch. In the forces of science, technology, industrialization and economy— and in the social patterns which develop through their influences, he sensed a striving for universality in our time and he accepted that as fact. 'I have tried to make an architecture for a technological society', he said, 'I have wanted to keep everything reasonable and clear—to have an architecture that anybody can do.

ARCHITECTURE AND CONSTRUCTION: Mies van der Rohe's knowledge of the possibilities and limitations of the materials with which we build—and particularly those which are typical and unique to our time such as rolled steel sections and large sheets of plate glass— enabled him to develop their respective potentialities as elements of construction to a level of poetic expression. Indeed, he thought of construction itself as being 'the truest guardian of the spirit of the times because it is objective and is not affected by personal individualism or fantasy'. So fundamental an aspect of architecture did he consider construction that he would often interpolate the German word *Baukunst* into discussions on the subject in order to further clarify his meaning. 'The *bau*', he would explain, 'is the clear building construction; while the *kunst* is the refinement of *that* and not anything more. Architecture begins when two bricks are put carefully together.'

1. Fifty foot by fifty foot house. Project: 1950–1.

2. Convention Hall. Project: 1953–4.

3. Drawing comparing plans of fifty foot by fifty foot house and 720 foot square Convention Hall.

The building illustrated on the left is 50 ft square; the one shown to its right is 720 ft square. Although they differ greatly in magnitude and in function—they are respectively a one-family house and a 50,000 seat convention hall—these two buildings clearly belong together and speak a single language.

Four reasons at least may be seen to have contributed towards this condition. *First:* Constructional clarity and athletic repose—characteristics associated with civil engineering more often than with architecture—have appeared through the removal of all unnecessary weight. 'We took all the unnecessary weight out of the buildings to make them as light as possible'. Mies van der Rohe said. 'It is often thought that heaviness is synonymous with strength. In my opinion

8

it is just the opposite.' *Second:* The materials used are industrially produced and the manner in which they are used acknowledges the specific nature of each. *Third:* The structural systems employed are in accordance with the requirements of the respective functions, and the components of these systems are revealed both internally and externally. *Fourth:* To complement this structural clarity, the enclosing skins and interior space dividers are separately defined from the stressed members, leaving no doubt as to what is structural and what is not.

For both the house and the convention hall, parallel generative impulses such as these have elicited a special kind of order; an order which permeates the whole building fabric, illuminating each part

as necessary and inevitable. This order should not be confused with that which is derived from mere constructional organization; rather, it may be more accurately described as the order of a structural organism.

The principle of structural order had been germane to all of the great architectural epochs. Being both morphological and organic it is a condition where *form becomes a consequence of structure and not the reason for the construction.* Mies van der Rohe believed that structure in this sense is a philosophical concept: 'The whole, from top to bottom, to the last detail, with the same ideas.'

The many different functional needs of our time contrast radically with the relative few of past epochs, and the absence of a general guiding principle in architecture today can only too easily produce environmental anarchy. In the principle of STRUCTURE Mies van der Rohe saw a universally tenable concept capable of embracing the diverse functional requirements of our epoch. 'The physicist Schrodinger', he pointed out, 'said of general principles that the creative vigour of a general principle depends precisely on its generality. And that is exactly what I mean when I talk about structure in architecture. It is not a special solution. It is a general idea. And although each building is a single solution, it is not motivated as such.'

In attempting to clarify this idea further, Mies van der Rohe often used the analogy of language: 'A living language can be used for normal day to day purposes as prose. If you are very good at that you may speak a wonderful prose. And if you are really good you can be a poet. But it is the same language, and its characteristic is that it has all these possibilities.'

While Mies van der Rohe believed that the same architectural language could be used for both a church and a factory, 'just as the Gothic men used the same principles for a cathedral as they would use for a barn', he emphasized that he would approach such diverse buildings in totally different ways: 'I would not build a church as I would a movie palace and I would not build a factory as I would a church, so that we make a clear distinction what the values of these buildings are. There is not only a hierarchy of values, there is a hierarchy of works too.'

In this respect St. Augustine's definition of 'order' was for Mies van der Rohe an important guiding concept. 'You have to realize', he would tell his students, 'that there are different stages of order. The real order is what St. Augustine said about the disposition of equal and unequal things according to their nature. That is real order. If you compare the Architects' Building (page 87) with the other I.I.T. campus buildings (page 73) you can see that. I think that the

Architects' Building is the most complete and the most refined building on the campus, and the most simple. In the other buildings there is more a practical order on a more economical level and in the Architects' Building it is a more spiritual order.'

In his youth Mies van der Rohe had shown great interest in the materials and construction of the many historic buildings which stood in his home town of Aachen. This interest gradually developed to form the basis from which his architectural philosophy evolved. 'It was at Berlage's Amsterdam Stock Exchange', he recalled of a visit to Holland in 1912, 'that the idea of a clear construction came to me as one of the fundamentals we should accept. We can talk about that easily, but to do it is not easy; it is very difficult to stick to this fundamental construction and then to elevate it to structure.'

During the course of a building's construction, when the structural skeleton is complete but still lacks the incrustations—and invariably the negations—of the 'architecture', it is impossible to remain unmoved by the clarity of the factual statement or the possibilities which could develop directly from it. Mies van der Rohe often drew his students' attention to the fact that the first flying buttresses were hidden under aisle roofs, they were considered merely constructional means for restraining the thrusts of the nave vaults. Later, when the vaults were lifted higher, and then higher still, the buttresses greatly increased in size and—since it now became difficult to hide them any longer—they were accepted as visual elements of the architecture. Thus, constructional necessity was translated into structural art.*

It is precisely this characteristic that distinguished Mies van der Rohe's work. It also formed the basis of his unique contribution as a pioneer in the field of modern architecture, for although he concentrated for almost half a century upon the development of a way of building which would reflect the scientific and technological society in which he was living, he never rejected the disciplines of STRUCTURAL architecture.

---

*This translation from constructional necessity was fundamental to all the great periods of architecture. For example, the development of the Romanesque basilica church into the Gothic cathedral was as equally attributable to the fervent belief of the Gothic mind in logical order and reasonability, or 'the postulate of clarification for clarification's sake', as Panofsky puts it, as to the transcendentalism of the Gothic idea. Since the builders of the 12th and 13th centuries lacked both the labour force and the transportation resources of the earlier times, their use of stone was conditioned by these limitations and as a result the optimum use to which comparatively small stone blocks were capable became the controlling factor of their architectural vocabulary.

In the domed Romanesque Church of St. Front at Perigueux (1120–50) the ratio of internal stone structure to volume of space enclosed is approximately 1 : 8. At Bourges Cathedral, built only just over half a century later, this ratio is 1 : 24. With

the same amount of stone three times as much space is enclosed. This radical change in the use of stone was made possible by the new balanced structural skeleton. And once this system had been established it was subjected to constant clarification and development. *The structural system set certain limitations and the possibilities existed only within these accepted facts.*

Evolution and inter-relationship of structure and space in Gothic architecture may be clearly studied at Lâon, through Bourges, to Amiens. At Lâon (1180) the space is cellular and, therefore, still somewhat Romanesque in character. At Bourges (1192), with the elimination of the transept, a new space is evolving. At Amiens (1200–35) by the integration of the individual spaces and their interpenetration the new concept fully emerges. Throughout this evolution, structure and space were interdependent and together eventually brought forth the great monotheistic image of the cathedral, a unity of structure, space and spirit.

4. Durham Cathedral—concealed flying buttresses.

5. Vézelay

6. Crown Hall, I.I.T. Chicago: 1950–6.

7. Carson, Pirie, Scott and Co. Chicago: 1899. Louis Sullivan, arch.

8. 860/880 Lake Shore Drive Apartments, Chicago: 1948–51.

9. Alumni Memorial Hall, I.I.T. Chicago: 1945–6. Construction photograph.

10. Alumni Memorial Hall, I.I.T.

11. Crown Hall, I.I.T. Chicago: 1950–6. Construction photograph.

12. Crown Hall, I.I.T.

13. 860/880 Lake Shore Drive Apartments, Chicago: 1948–51. Construction photograph.

15. Fifty foot by fifty foot square house. Project: 1950–1.

14. 860/880 Lake Shore Drive Apartments.

16. Convention Hall. Project: 1953–4.

Structural and Spatial Concepts

Prior to the Industrial Revolution, the principal building material had been masonry—a fact that resulted in space being defined by structure. With the arrival of the iron and steel ages it became possible, for the first time, to separate the structural elements from the space-defining elements. The great exhibition halls, the railway station sheds and the conservatories were the first building types to put the new materials to significant use. But architects in general were reluctant to break with the old historical eclecticisms for any buildings other than those of a strictly utilitarian nature. For these buildings—factories and commercial structures in the main—the new materials and means were often applied and expressed in direct and honest ways, and in demonstrating new architectural possibilities they pointed the way towards the development of an architecture based completely upon the evolving technology.

By the early 1920's the first signs of the new architecture developing a broader base began to appear in Europe. At this time Mies van der Rohe—who was then in his mid-thirties—prepared a series of projects in which he studied the architectural potential of the new materials and methods. These projects inferred proposals of a general nature, and since all of his subsequent work developed logically under their influence, it is essential that they should be discussed before we begin to examine the main body of his work.

17. The Great Exhibition Building, London: 1851. Sir Joseph Paxton.

18. The Great Exhibition Building, London: 1851.

19. The Great Stove, Chatsworth: 1836. Sir Joseph Paxton.

20. Euston Station, London: 1835–9.

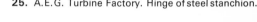

21. Gum Department Store, Moscow: 1893. Alexander Pomeranzen, architect.

22. Studebaker Building, Chicago: 1895. S. S. Beman, architect.

23. Beurs, Amsterdam: 1898–1903. H. P. Berlage, architect.

24. A.E.G. Turbine Factory, Berlin: 1909. Peter Behrens, architect.

25. A.E.G. Turbine Factory. Hinge of steel stanchion.

Three Projects: 1922-3

GLASS SKYSCRAPER: 1922

Mies van der Rohe's interest in glass as a building material led him to prepare a number of studies in which large glass surfaces were used as the major part of a non load-bearing peripheral enclosure. Studies for the Glass Skyscraper of 1922 were made by setting up narrow strips of glass in a plasticine base so as to form various contours. In this way the reflective qualities of the material could be examined. The structure was behind the glass—within the building.

CONCRETE OFFICE BUILDING: 1923

In contrast to the Glass Skyscraper, the Concrete Office Building, a year later, emphatically and eloquently proclaimed its structural guts. Here, the structural system was dominant—it was the architecture. And to prevent any dilution of this basic idea, the glass window plane was pushed back to the interior face of the up-turned floor slab—a feature which formed a continuous enclosure for storage units around the building's perimeter. Mies van der Rohe recalled that when he was working on this project he was, '. . . a little inspired by the Palazzo Pitti, for I wanted to see if we could make something of a similar strength with our means and for our purposes'.

BRICK COUNTRY HOUSE: 1923

The decellularization of interior space had appeared in its germinal form at Frank Lloyd Wright's Oak Park residence of 1889, and although Wright continued to develop this idea in his subsequent work, by the time he built the Martin House in 1904 he appears to have advanced its possibilities as far as he felt it was necessary. A further development of this idea was, however, initiated with the introduction of the completely free-standing wall in Mies van der Rohe's 1923 project for a Brick Country House.

In this work the walls were treated as clearly defined individual load-bearing entities, placed in a semi-overlapping manner in order that any one area of the house was not rigidly enclosed, but rather subtly defined in its relation with other areas. By this decellularization, the space flowed freely as a continuum throughout the house, and since walls were often pulled out beyond the roof plane into the landscape, the defining line between interior and exterior was minimized. This liberation of interior space was developed further in 1929 at the Barcelona Pavilion.

Mies van der Rohe described the ideas underlying his glass skyscraper projects in FRÜHLICHT, 1922:

Skyscrapers reveal their bold structural pattern during construction. Only then does the gigantic steel web seem impressive. When the outer walls are put in place, the structural system which is the basis of all artistic design, is hidden by a chaos of meaningless and trivial forms. When finished, these buildings are impressive only because of their size; yet they could surely be more than mere examples of our technical ability. Instead of trying to solve the new problems with old forms, we should develop the new forms from the very nature of the new problems.

We can see the new structural principles most clearly when we use glass in place of the outer walls, which is feasible today since in a skeleton building these outer walls do not actually carry weight. The use of glass imposes new solutions.

In my project for a skyscraper at the Friedrichstrasse Station in Berlin I used a prismatic form which seemed to me to fit best the triangular site of the building. I placed the glass walls at slight angles to each other to avoid the monotony of over-large glass surfaces.

I discovered by working with actual glass models that the important thing is the play of reflections and not the effect of light and shadow as in ordinary buildings.

The results of these experiments can be seen in the second scheme published here. At first glance the curved outline of the plan seems arbitrary. These curves, however, were determined by three factors: sufficient illumination of the interior, the massing of the building viewed from the street, and lastly the play of reflections. I proved in the glass model that calculations of light and shadow do not help in designing an all-glass building.

The only fixed points of the plan are the stair and elevator shafts. All the other elements of the plan fit the needs of the building and are designed to be carried out in glass.

Describing his Concrete Office Building project in G, No. 1—1923 Mies van der Rohe wrote:

The office building is a house of work, of organization, of clarity, of economy.

Broad, light workspace, unbroken, but articulated according to the organization of the work. Maximum effect with minimum means.

The materials: concrete, steel, glass.

Reinforced concrete structures are skeletons by nature. No gingerbread. No fortress. Columns and girders eliminate bearing walls. This is skin and bone construction.

Functional division of the work space determines the width of the building: 16 meters. The most economic system was found to be two rows of columns spanning 8 meters with 4 meters cantilevered on either side. The girders are spaced 5 meters apart. These girders carry the floor slabs, which at the end of the cantilevers are turned up perpendicularly to form the outer skin of the building. Cabinets are placed against these walls in order to permit free visibility in the center of the rooms. Above the cabinets, which are 2 meters high, runs a continuous band of windows.

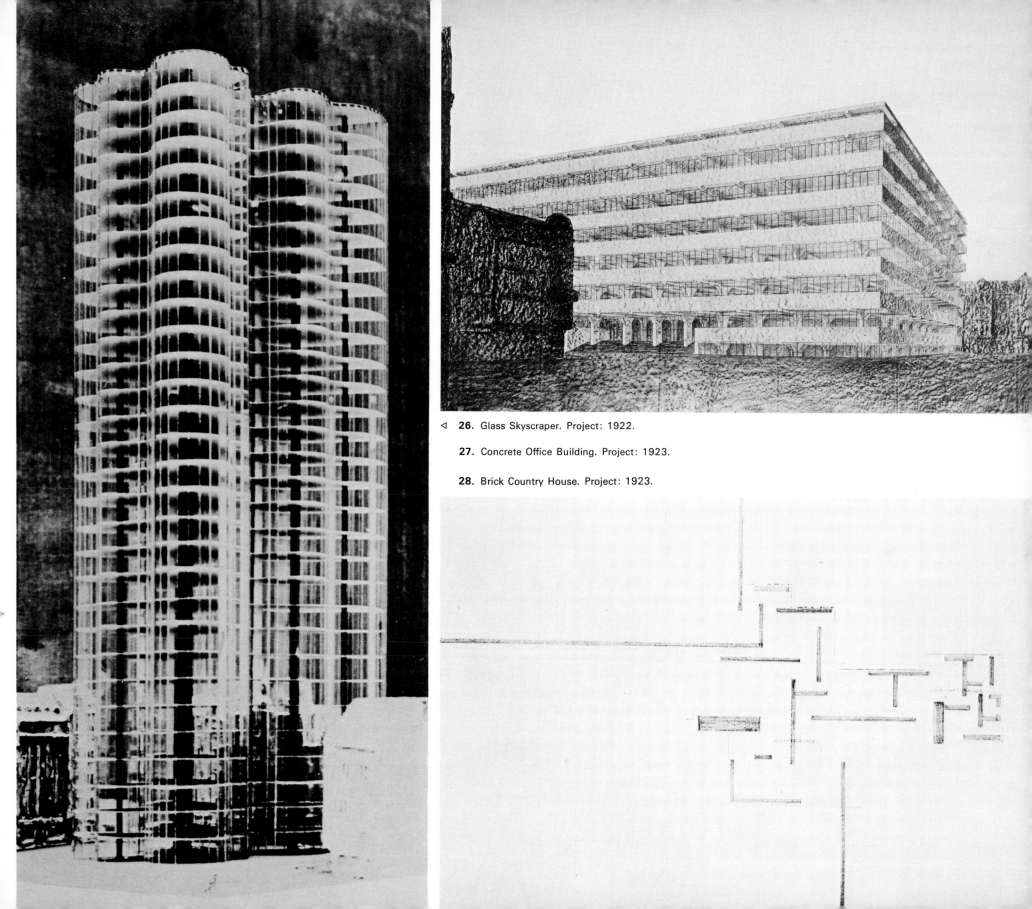

◁ **26.** Glass Skyscraper. Project: 1922.

27. Concrete Office Building. Project: 1923.

28. Brick Country House. Project: 1923.

Two Seminal Buildings: 1928–30

A decade after the projects of the 1920's, Mies van der Rohe built two structures which may, in retrospect, be seen as providing a master key to the understanding of his subsequent work. He had already begun to make preliminary studies for one of these buildings —the Tugendhat House—when he was asked to design and build within the following six months a pavilion to represent Germany at the 1929 International Exposition in Barcelona. While he was concentrating upon the planning of this pavilion he suddenly became aware, as if after years of rumination, that structural elements and space-defining elements could be separate entities, and by being so would release a new and significant architectural force.

In the Brick Country House project, the free-standing walls had fulfilled both load-bearing and space-defining functions. The walls of the Barcelona Pavilion and also those on the main floor of the Tugendhat House, however, were set free of structural obligation; they were purely space-defining elements freely located within the regular framework of an open structural skeleton. To emphasize this separation of functions, the walls were often placed only a few inches away from the structural columns. Spatially, no part of these plans was closed, but instead, each area became a natural part of adjacent areas. The space was fluid and contiguous and, in contrast to the traditional compartmentalized plan, the greater whole could be sensed although not actually seen.

With the successful application of these ideas to the different functional requirements of the Barcelona Pavilion and the Tugendhat House, Mies van der Rohe was convinced that he had arrived at a sound general principle upon which to develop his future work.

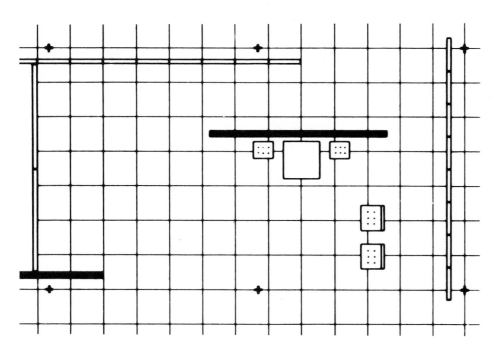

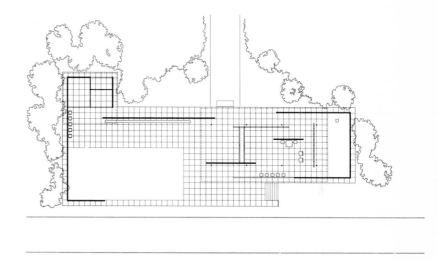

30. German Pavilion, International Exposition, Barcelona: 1928–9. Detail from plan.

31. German Pavilion, International Exposition, Barcelona. Plan.

32. Tugendhat House, Brno, Czechoslovakia: 1928–30. Detail from plan.

33. Tugendhat House, Brno, Czechoslovakia. Plan.

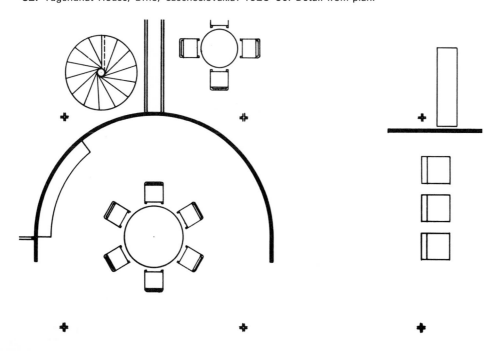

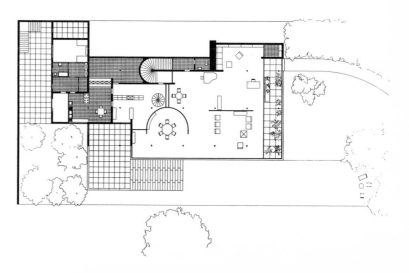

BARCELONA PAVILION: 1928–9

Mies van der Rohe and Lilly Reich were jointly responsible for the design of the German section of the 1929 International Exposition at Barcelona; when France and Britain decided to build national pavilions at the exposition, the German government commissioned Mies van der Rohe to prepare the design of a similarly representative structure. In addition to being open to the general public, this pavilion would accommodate the inaugural ceremonies of the exposition's German section (attended by the King and Queen of Spain) and be used for numerous government receptions.

The site selected was crossed by one of the exposition's walking routes. By allowing this path to continue uninterrupted through the spaces of his building, Mies van der Rohe underlined the open character of those spaces and eased the transition between the exterior and interior.

The pavilion consisted of two horizontal planes: the smaller—forming the roof, being held above the larger—forming a raised terrace, by cruciform shaped steel columns. Freely placed between these two planes were non-load-bearing walls of marble and glass; some extending beyond the roof plane to enclose and articulate exterior spaces.

Because there was very little time available for the design and construction of this building, as soon as Mies van der Rohe had decided upon its basic concept, he set about locating marble for one of the free-standing walls. He recalled that it was winter at the time '. . . since you cannot move marble in from the quarry in winter because it is still wet inside and would easily freeze and break into pieces, we had to find dry material. Eventually I found an onyx block of a certain size, and since I only had the possibility of this block, I made the pavilion twice that height, and then we developed the plan.'

◁ **34.** German Pavilion, International Exposition, Barcelona, 1928–9. Court with pool and sculpture (Kolbe).

35. German Pavilion, International Exposition, Barcelona. View from rear terrace looking into sculpture court.

The richness of the materials used in the pavilion: the marble and onyx walls, the travertine-faced podium, the tinted glass and the chromium-plated column covers—with the attendant transparency and reflectivity producing a fantasy of complex ambiguity, has frequently blinded critics to the significant architectural values of this work. Namely: A clearly expressed separation between structural and non-structural elements; a free and open plan; a completely new kind of space. These qualities may be appreciated even from a brief examination of the photographs and drawings of this building, and they are the characteristics to which the architect would refer whenever he discussed the building.

At Barcelona Mies van der Rohe brought his ideas on structure and space to a remarkable synthesis. From horizontal and vertical planes, opaque and transparent materials and skeletal construction, he created a building of great poetic feeling, whose position in terms of architectural development is undeniably that of a seminal work.

A contemporary newspaper account pointed out that '. . . while the average visitor will find the building difficult to understand, for those who are artistically sensitive to the modern feeling, it becomes a rewarding adventure. The absolute material austerity of the enclosed space is impregnated with a harmony of colours and forms. Viewing Kolbe's sculpture, which stands in the court pool, through the green tinted glass wall produces a feeling of noble calm and sublime tranquillity. This building of marble and glass by the architect Mies van der Rohe provides the visitor with a peaceful refuge from the busy and crowded grounds of the exhibition.'

Mies van der Rohe wished to use furniture in the pavilion which, although it would have to be somewhat monumental in character because it would be used by the King and Queen of Spain during the inaugural ceremonies, would also complement the building and not block its spatial flow by being too solid in appearance. Since no suitable pieces were available, he designed the well-known Barcelona chair, stool and table for this purpose.

The possibility of establishing a complementary relationship between sculpture and architecture is a recurrent concern with architects. However, sculpture would seem to attain a significant architectural value only when acting directly on the milieu—as exemplified by the Athena on the Acropolis, or, when no longer an appendage, it exists as a fully integrated element of the architecture—as was the case with the opulent surface modelling of the Baroque. At Barcelona, Mies van der Rohe introduced sculpture into his pavilion in a manner not dissimilar to Balthasar Neumann's brilliantly sophisticated use of the oval central altar at Vierzehnheiligen. For just as Neumann used a sculptural object as a means of penetration for his explosive spatial movements into the central area of his church, so Mies van der Rohe, at Barcelona, used the Kolbe figure as a necessary and integral part of his pavilion's space movement character. So perfectly was this sculpture in sympathy with the pavilion's scale and spatial flow, and its location so important as a point of reference, that it comes as somewhat of a surprise to learn that it was an existing work, and not one commissioned especially for the pavilion. In fact, Mies van der Rohe did not normally agree with the idea of commissioning sculpture for a building. When he felt that sculpture could make a positive contribution, he preferred to select an existing piece because it could be tested for its suitability—in terms of scale and its relationship to the architecture—before a final decision was made.

36. German Pavilion, International Exposition, Barcelona. Interior view with free-standing onyx wall.

37. German Pavilion, International Exposition, Barcelona. View from terrace.

38. German Pavilion, International Exposition, Barcelona. Exterior view.

39. German Pavilion, International Exposition, Barcelona. View of Pavilion from main terrace.

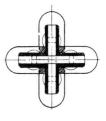

40. Tugendhat House, Brno, Czechoslovakia: 1928–30. View from the garden.

41. Tugendhat House. View of main floor at glass wall. 42. Tugendhat House. Interior view of main floor.

43. Tugendhat House. Interior view of main floor. 44. Tugendhat House. View of dining area on main floor.

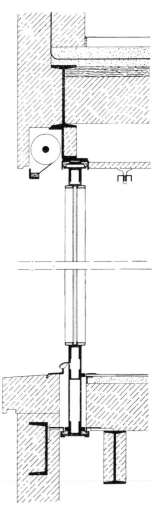

45. Tugendhat House. Detail of column cover.

46. Tugendhat House. Section through lowerable glass wall.

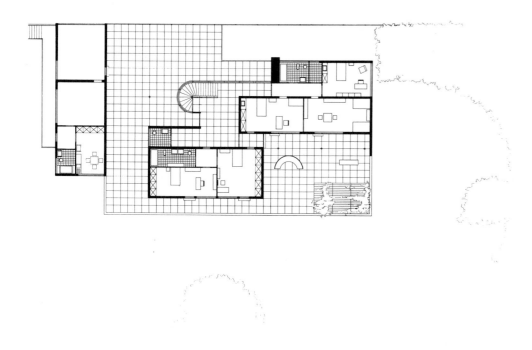

TUGENDHAT HOUSE: 1928–30

47. Tugendhat House. Plan of upper level (street entrance).

48. Tugendhat House. Plan of main living level.

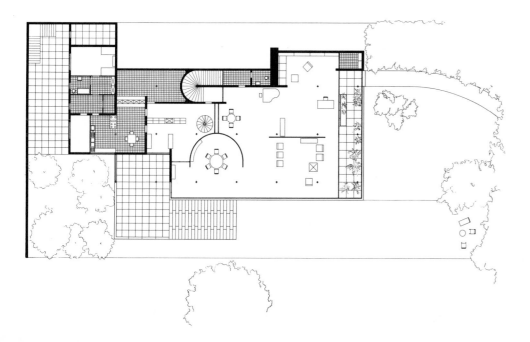

By planning this house on two levels, Mies van der Rohe was able to take full advantage of the site's steep slope. On the upper and street entrance level, three rectangular enclosures accommodate respectively the master bedroom suite, the children's rooms, and the garage and chauffeur's quarters. The overlapping placement of these three volumes suggests spatial relationships to be seen later at the Weissenhofsiedlung in Stuttgart (page 115) and at the campus of Illinois Institute of Technology in Chicago (page 115).

The plan of the house's lower level is of particular interest, because it consists principally of a single 50 ft by 80 ft space within which dining, library and general living areas are subtly articulated by free-standing walls placed independently of the column system. This space was provided with extensive glass walls which could be lowered into the basement in order to permit maximum contact with the exterior.

The Tugendhat House—in common with the Barcelona Pavilion—incorporated materials of the finest quality. Gold and white onyx and Macassar ebony for the free-standing walls defining, respectively, the living and dining areas, are typical examples. Mies van der Rohe also continued the traditional European practice of designing almost every piece of furniture and equipment for the house; it was for this building that he designed the now widely used 'Brno' and 'Tugendhat' chairs.

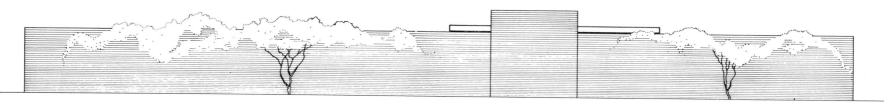

49. House with three courts. Project: 1934.

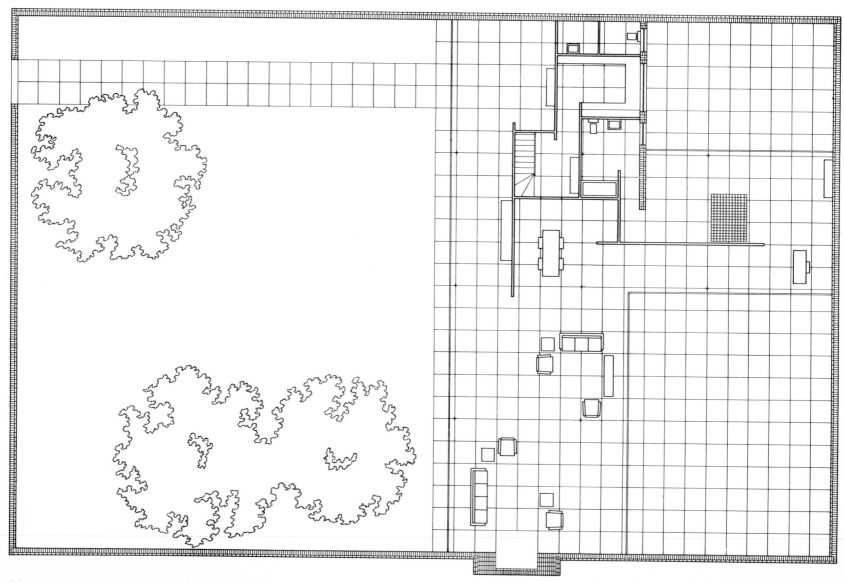

The intensity with which Mies van der Rohe investigated the possibilities of the direction initiated by the Barcelona Pavilion and the Tugendhat House is illustrated by projects for buildings of totally different function and magnitude:

50. Hubbe House, Magdeburg, Germany. Project: 1935. Living room.

51. Group of Three Court Houses. Project: 1938.

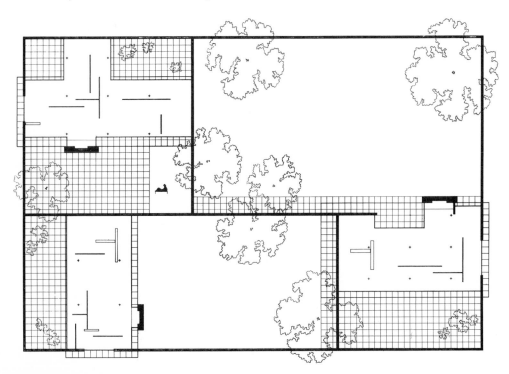

COURT HOUSES: 1931–8

The structural and spatial characteristics of Barcelona re-appear—contained within a peripheral brick wall—in a series of studies for single-storey court houses made during the years 1931–8. Houses with one, two and three courts were planned, and group and row assembly proposed. The free-standing walls under a floating roof plane gave great spatial richness, even to a small house. Mies van der Rohe believed that the essential character of these houses was made possible by the large sheets of glass which allowed every space and building element to be perceived almost simultaneously; he thought that the court house in this form would be an ideal solution for the urban residence (page 122).

52. Resor House, Jackson Hole, Wyoming. Project: 1938. Exterior view.

53. Resor House. View of landscape from living room.

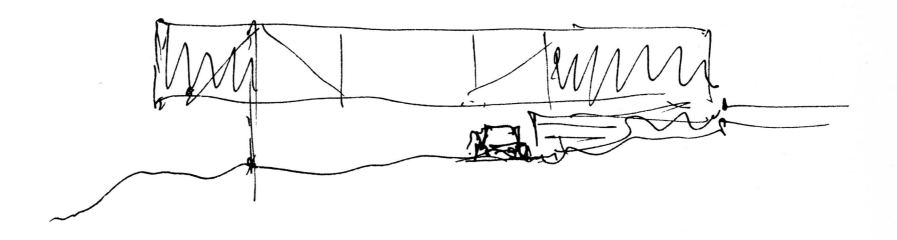

RESOR HOUSE: 1938

The site selected for this house at Jackson Hole, Wyoming extended across a narrow river and enjoyed unimpeded views of the Grand Teton Mountains. The house was conceived as a bridge over the river, with the bedroom suite located at one end and the service accommodation at the other end; in between these two closed areas was a large open living space in which free-standing walls and furniture elements articulated particular activities in a manner not dissimilar to that already developed at the Tugendhat House. While the Resor House project of 1938 may be said to have certain antecedents at Brno, its simple volumetric form and the manner in which this was emphasized through its physical detachment from the terrain anticipated the Farnsworth House of 1947 (page 83). In this context, it is interesting to note that the sketch which Mies van der Rohe made in 1934 for a 'Glass House on a Hillside' illustrates the first occasion on which he had proposed such detachment from the ground.

54. Glass House on a Hillside. Project: 1934.

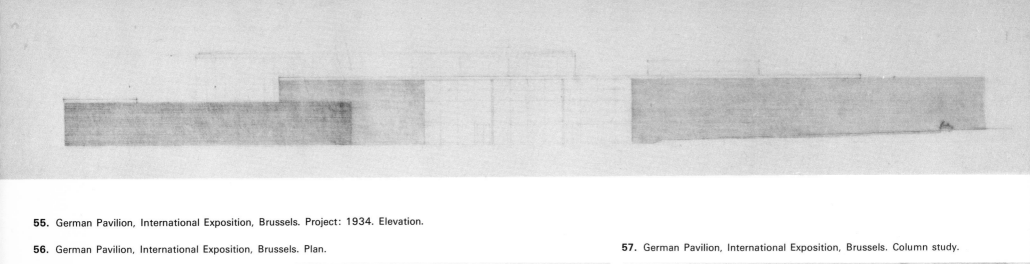

55. German Pavilion, International Exposition, Brussels. Project: 1934. Elevation.

56. German Pavilion, International Exposition, Brussels. Plan.

57. German Pavilion, International Exposition, Brussels. Column study.

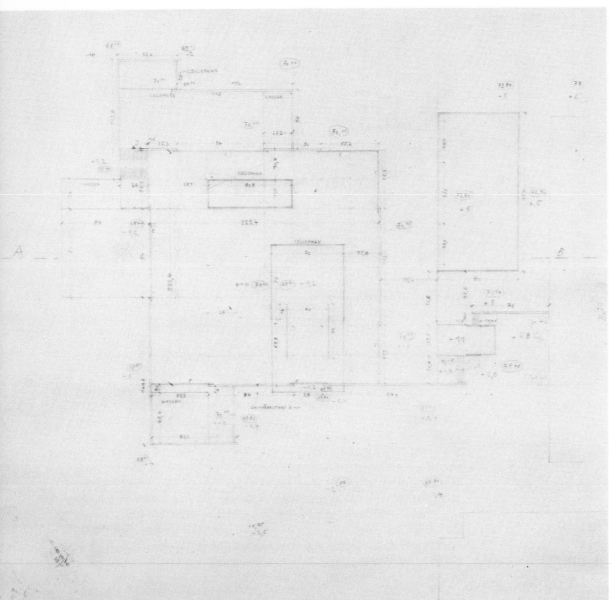

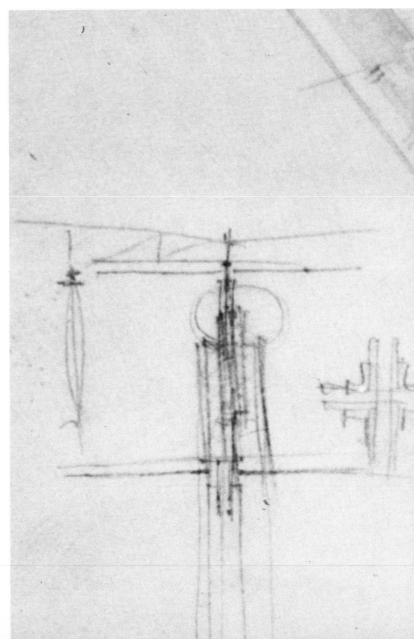

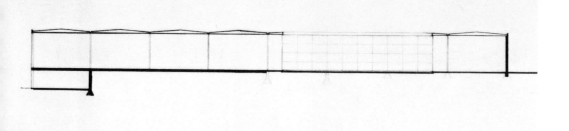

58. German Pavilion, International Exposition, Brussels. Section.

59. German Pavilion, International Exposition, Brussels. Interior view showing garden court.

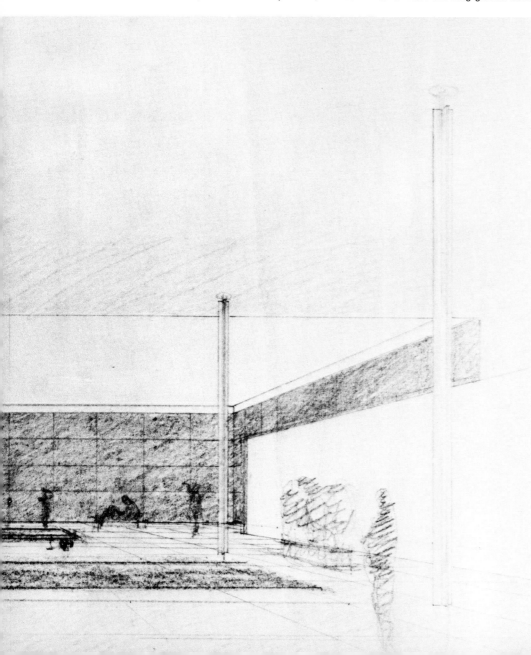

This vast 222.4 metres (729 ft 6 in) square exhibition pavilion would have been Mies van der Rohe's contribution to the projected International Exposition of 1934. The building's plan was based upon a square structural bay established by column spacings of 28 metres (91 ft 10 in); eight of these bays in each direction support a roof structure that is held 16 metres (52 ft 6 in) above the floor. The pavilion's non-loadbearing enclosing walls consisted of glass and brick panels; the brick often extending beyond the building's roof to embrace exterior terraces and pools.

Internally, the space was subdivided by two open courts placed in the semi-overlapping manner that had, by this time, become intrinsic to Mies van der Rohe's concept of a freely flowing and functionally flexible space contained within the framework of a regular structural system.

While the Brussels Pavilion project illustrates the application on a greater scale of principles set at Barcelona and Brno, this building will also be recognized as a precursor of many of Mies van der Rohe's subsequent works in America—the I.I.T. Library and Administration Building, for example (page 76); and particularly of his series of clear-span universal-space halls (page 79).

Structural and Spatial Concepts—Summary

During the development of Mies van der Rohe's structural and spatial concepts, one dominant architectural idea—*that of the separation of the structural from the space-defining elements*—suddenly emerged. While Mies van der Rohe was certainly not alone in sensing the possibilities of structural and spatial independence, his growing concern for structural clarity uniquely positioned him for the task of extracting an architectural principle from these possibilities. In this context, the pavilion at Barcelona and the house in Brno represented both the culmination of his studies in this direction—the moment at which the significance of these ideas first become apparent to him— as well as the point of departure for his future work.

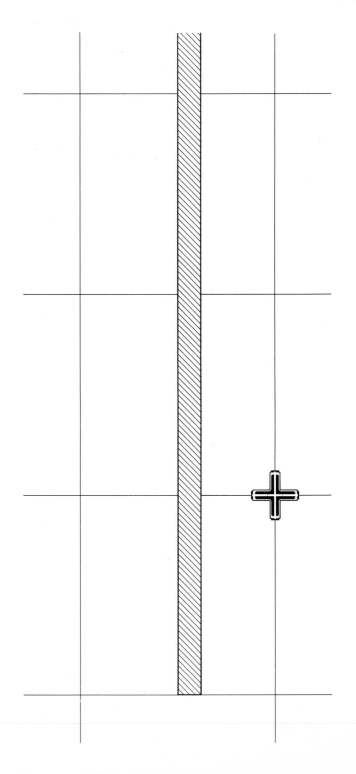

60. A column and free-standing wall from the Barcelona Pavilion (1928)—the first example of the architectural potential inherent in the separation of structural elements from space-defining elements.

61. Tugendhat House, Brno, Czechoslovakia: 1928–30. ▷

Three Building Types

The dictum that form follows function was first stated as an architectural credo by Louis Sullivan in the 1890's. Mies van der Rohe, however, believed that functional requirements may, in time, change, while form, once rigidly established, cannot easily be modified. He therefore chose a structural system in relation to the magnitude of the functional requirements as a whole rather than to their individual and specific needs. And because he was convinced that the principle of flexibility was a modern principle, he fixed only essentials in his buildings, thereby permitting great flexibility and freedom for both initial layouts and future modifications.

Considered from the standpoint of a taxonomic analysis, functions may be grouped according to their general space requirements, and these space requirements may be satisfied within the feasible economic range of particular structural types. It follows, therefore, that if an optimum operable level is to be achieved for a function, this will best be realized by its accommodation within a particular structural type. It also follows, that if functions which call for totally different space requirements (i.e. a banking hall and an office building) are forced into a structural type that is appropriate only to one, each function could as a result be penalized.

It is this morphological approach to the accommodation of function that was central to Mies van der Rohe's concentration upon three specific building types: the high-rise skeleton frame building; the low-rise skeleton frame building; and the single-storey clear-span building. The purpose of this section of the book is to analyse in turn each of these building types through an examination of their planning characteristics, their structural systems, and the methods employed for their enclosure.

High-rise Skeleton Frame Buildings

That the predominant characteristic of a low-rise building is horizontal spread, while that of a high-rise building is vertical extension, is obvious enough. Nevertheless, with this assertion, one is calling attention to their respective possibilities and limitations with regard to such aspects as site, function, structure, services and elevatoring. In a low-rise building, for example, the influence of the latter two considerations upon the plan is minimal, while for a high-rise building they are of crucial importance if a balanced plan and an economical structural bay is to be achieved. In Mies van der Rohe's multi-storey skeletal buildings—whether they accommodate offices or apartments—only the transportation and service shafts are fixed. The open structural frame* provides a free space allowing particular needs to be individually satisfied.

*In order to take full advantage of the flexibility in planning permitted by a regularly organized structural frame, a clear resolution of the problems caused by wind loads is imperative. Mies van der Rohe's use of reinforced concrete flat and waffle slab construction was confined to office and apartment buildings of no more than 30 stories in height and where minimum costs were paramount. In such cases, the problem of wind load was resolved by stiffening the structure through the introduction of shear walls in the core areas.

For his steel-framed structures, the solution was relative to the magnitude of the building. As a general rule, for steel-framed buildings of about the size of the 26-storey 860 Lake Shore Drive apartments (page 53), it is structurally possible and economically feasible to transfer wind loads to the building's foundations through the stiffening of the structural frame by appropriate design of all column/girder connections.

Buildings of greater magnitude require a different resolution of this problem, and in such cases the introduction of bracing in the central bays—on the column lines between elevator shafts and other core accommodation—will provide stiffness and permit wind loads to be collected and transferred to the foundations in an economical and practical manner. This solution, however, requires further development when a building reaches the magnitude of the 56-storey Toronto Dominion Bank Tower (page 65). In this case, in order to fall below the maximum sway limitations of ·002 times the height of the building, a series of cantilevered trusses extend from the braced core bays to the peripheral columns at the intermediate mechanical levels to make the full width of the building effective against overturning.

(Steel-framed buildings of greater magnitude than the Toronto Dominion Bank Tower will require a different structural concept. In recent years a solution to this new problem considers a tower's periphery as forming the walls of a tube, often through the introduction of diagonal bracing elements.)

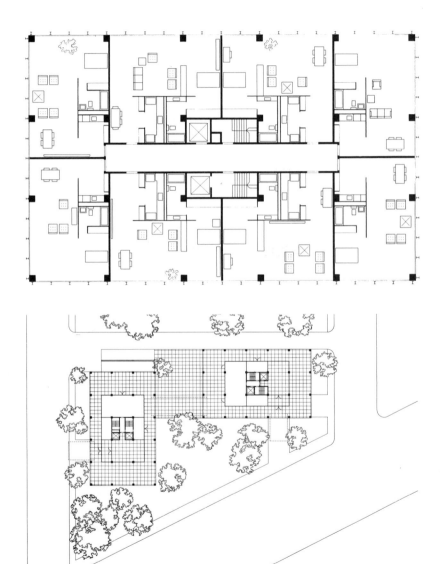

62. 860/880 Lake Shore Drive Apartments, Chicago: 1948–51. Typical apartment floor plan.

63. 860–880 Lake Shore Drive Apartments. Street level plan.

64. 860–880 Lake Shore Drive Apartments. Construction photograph. ▷

HIGH-RISE BUILDINGS: OFFICES

In order to determine the type and the dimensions of a structural system suitable for a multi-storey, variegated tenancy office building, it is necessary to consider the following factors in addition to those of an economical nature and to interpret them within the context of the particular site.

Room sizes: The minimum width for a single person office is usually between 9 ft and 10 ft; a more desirable office would be around 15 ft. The accumulation of these office increments in various sequences becomes a guide for determining the size of the structural bay and also the building's module.

Elevatoring: For elevatoring purposes, a multi-storey building is divided into groups of consecutive floors, i.e. low-rise, intermediate-rise, high-rise. The number of these rises is determined by the standard of elevatoring service that is considered desirable for the building's occupancy. In turn, the number of elevators in each rise or bank relates to the number of people who are working on a typical floor served by that bank. Thus, for example, if eight 4,000 lbs capacity elevators are needed, two shafts, each in the region of 10 ft by 40 ft separated by a lobby space, will be required. involving a total space allotment of around 30 ft by 40 ft.

Clear floor to ceiling height: Since economic factors are the principal influences in determining this dimension, the range lies between the minimum acceptable by code and the desirable maximum relative to the building's type of occupancy.

Floor depth: This dimension is determined by the minimum depth that is possible with regard to structural economy, horizontal mechanical service distribution, and the code requirements.

For the majority of his multi-storey office buildings, Mies van der Rohe utilized the steel skeleton frame because he believed that it would satisfy these requirements in an efficient and economical way; moreover, it was a proven structural system and one which could provide a maximum of unobstructed floor space—and consequently great flexibility for the planning of offices. The structural bay of these steel skeletons is usually between 30 ft by 30 ft and 30 ft by 40 ft, with a floor to floor dimension of around 12 ft (i.e. 9 ft clear floor to ceiling and 3 ft overall floor depth). The subdivision of the structural bay into modules of around 5 ft—or a dimension similarly related to the interior functional requirements as noted above—sets the positions and frequency of perimeter air conditioning units, ceiling lighting/air handling fixtures, floor outlets for electrical and telephone connections, floor to ceiling partitions, as well as for the mullion divisions of the building's enclosing skin.

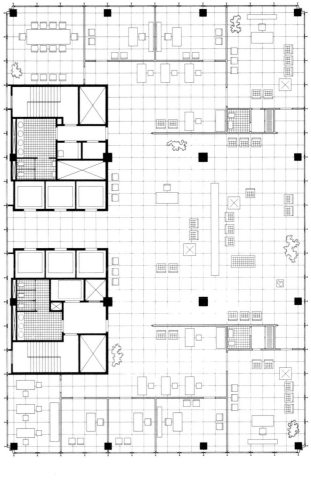

65. A New City Square and Office Tower, London: 1967–. Plan of typical office floor.

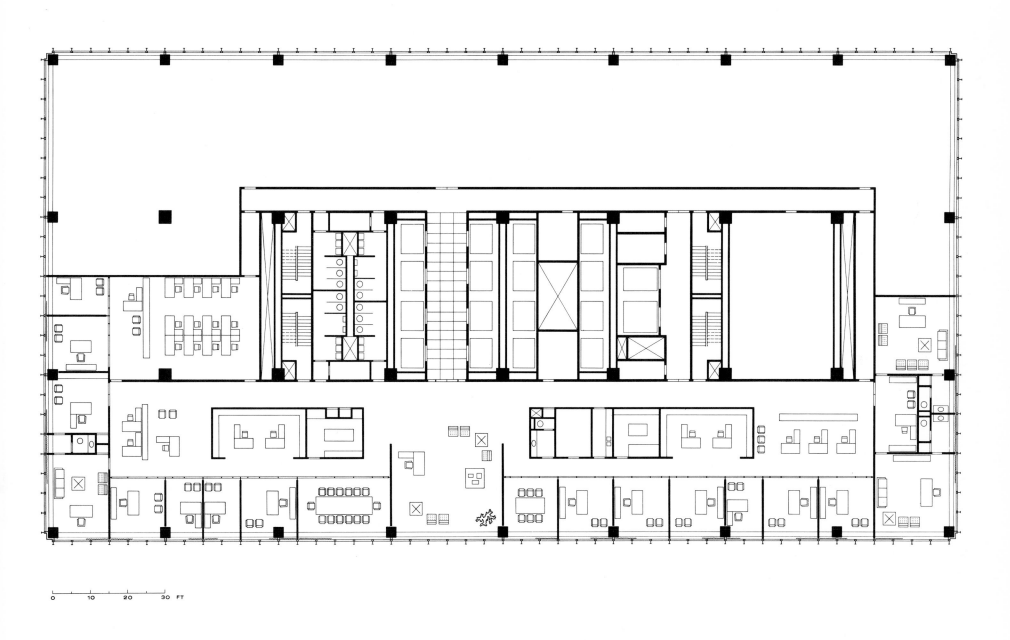

66. Toronto Dominion Bank Tower, Toronto: 1963–7. Office plan for Cemp Investments Limited and The Fairview Corporation Limited on the 33rd floor.

106949

In Mies van der Rohe's multi-storey office buildings, those functions which are shared by tenants—such as elevators, fire stairs and toilets —and those which relate to building management and mechanical services—such as janitor's closets, telephone and electrical rooms and duct shafts—are gathered together into central cores with each function located in a straight vertical line in order to avoid jogs. This centralization of the fixed and repetitive functions leaves the surrounding perimeter floor area free for subdivision into corridor and office spaces as particular requirements dictate.

A depth of around 40 ft between the core and the building's perimeter has proved to be an optimum for economical office planning. When the site conditions were too restrictive to permit this, as was the case with the Mansion House Square office tower in London (page 147), precedence was given to the provision of workable office space and the cores were located in positions which permitted this.

The ground floors of Mies van der Rohe's office buildings are usually around 26 ft clear in height and are enclosed by glass walls set well back from the building's perimeter. The only solid elements at this level are cores which house the elevators, fire stairs and service shafts; the remaining area functions as entrance space, affording access to the building from every direction. These high and open ground floors provide the buildings with entrances which are inviting, and in scale with the building's magnitude and with the number of people who use it; furthermore, their very openness tends to lighten the visual weight of the mass above by allowing the city space to flow through at ground level.

67. Toronto Dominion Bank Tower, Toronto: 1963–7. Office interior for Cemp Investments Limited and The Fairview Corporation Limited on the 33rd floor.

68. Toronto Dominion Bank Tower, Toronto: 1963–7. Ground floor entrance lobby.

69. Toronto Dominion Bank Tower, Toronto: 1963–7. Reception area of the offices for Cemp Investments Limited and The Fairview Corporation Limited on the 33rd floor.

71. Toronto Dominion Bank Tower. Interior of ground floor entrance lobby.

70. Toronto Dominion Bank Tower, Toronto: 1963–7. Reception area of the offices for Cemp Investments Limited and The Fairview Corporation Limited on the 33rd floor.

72. Toronto Dominion Bank Tower. Typical floor elevator lobby.

In apartment buildings the technical problems are far less complicated than in office buildings. The mechanical services, for example, consist basically of vertical risers; a deep and open floor construction would not, therefore, be an advantage. On the contrary, it would add unnecessary height to the building. The type of construction and the dimensions of the structural bay will be influenced by the desirable widths and depths of the two major apartment spaces: the living room and the bedroom, and generally these will allow for a smaller, more economical bay than is feasible for the typical office building. For a typical apartment building Mies van der Rohe found that a flat slab reinforced concrete structure, with a bay of around 21 ft square, a floor depth of 9 in, and a clear floor to ceiling height of around 8 ft would satisfy the requirements from both economic and planning standpoints. Furthermore, the subdivision of the 21 ft structural bay into 5 ft 3 in or 10 ft 6 in modules (dimensions which relate to the living room and bedroom widths) provided a convenient unit for the building's enclosing skin.

To achieve an optimum width for an apartment building, Mies van der Rohe planned the typical floor with a central access corridor surrounded by a compact ring of accommodation comprising the building's elevators, fire stairs and service shafts, and the apartments' kitchens and bathrooms—all functions for which daylight is not essential. With these fixed and repetitive elements confined to the centre of each floor, the peripheral unimpeded area is released for subdivision into living spaces.

As with his office buildings, the ground floors of Mies van der Rohe's apartment buildings are kept as open as possible. Usually the only solid elements are the cores which house the elevators, fire stairs and service shafts; the remaining area is developed as entrance lobby, lounge and occasionally commissary or service space. Again, the ground floor is high—usually in the region of 16 ft—with the enclosing glass wall set well back from the building's perimeter, making an inviting entrance to the building.

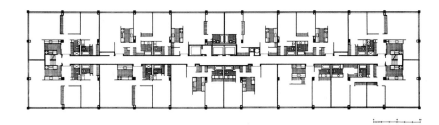

73. Highfield House, Apartment Building, Baltimore: 1963–5. Typical apartment floor plan.

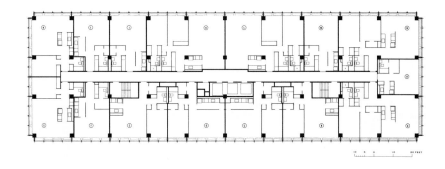

74. Lafayette Towers, Lafayette Park, Detroit: 1963. Typical apartment floor plan.

75. Highfield House, Apartment Building. Ground floor entrance lobby.

76. Highfield House, Apartment Building. Exterior view.

77. Lafayette Towers. Apartment interior showing housing for heating pipes and optional air-conditioner.

78. Lafayette Towers. Exterior view.

HIGH-RISE BUILDINGS: THREE SKIN SOLUTIONS

(1) In this, the first of the three types of enclosure solution which Mies van der Rohe employed for high-rise buildings, the skin becomes an infill between the columns and floor beams. This solution may be seen at the Promontory Apartments in Chicago, 1946–9, and at Highfield House Apartments in Baltimore, 1963–5. Both buildings are of reinforced concrete construction, and the skin infill consists of a panel of fixed and openable windows set above a brick spandrel.

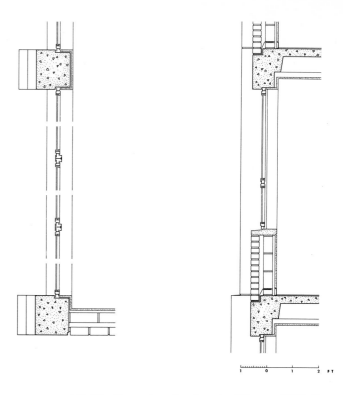

79–80. Promontory Apartments, Chicago: 1946–9.

(2) In this enclosure solution for steel skeleton framed buildings, the glass is set between the structural frame with its exterior face contiguous with the steel cover plates of the columns and edge beams. The introduction of projecting steel mullions at the module points, including where the columns occur, has caused the structural frame and its glass infill to become architecturally fused—each element losing a part of its particular identity in the process of establishing a single architectural statement. (When perimeter columns and floor beams are exposed to the elements, they are subject to different temperature conditions from those structural members which are located within the building. While these interior members remain static, the perimeter members will expand and contract in accordance with exterior temperature variations. In very tall buildings the accumulation of these movements to beyond the critical point may require the introduction of special structural and insulation treatments.)

An example of this solution may be seen at the 860 Lake Shore Drive Apartments in Chicago, 1948–51, where the skin consists of steel mullions, column covers, and floor and roof fascia plates—painted matte black; aluminium glazing frames with openable hoppers; and clear plate glass. Assembly: the skin was fabricated on the building's roof in two-storey high, 21 ft widths, and lowered into position (page 53).

Another application of this skin solution may be seen at the Science Center of Duquesne University in Pittsburgh, 1962–8. Here the skin consists of steel mullions, column covers, floor and roof fascia plates, glazing frames. and under-window panels—painted matte black; and bronze-grey tinted glass. Assembly: the skin was assembled on the building from separate elements, i.e. column covers, floor fascia plates, mullions and one module wide subframes with under-window panels in position.

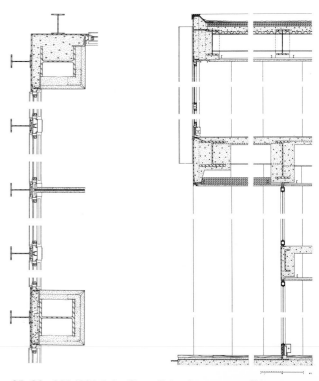

85–86. 860/880 Lake Shore Drive Apartments, Chicago: 1948–51.

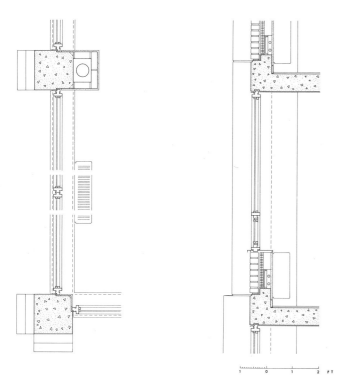

83. Promontory Apartments.

84. Highfield House Apartments.

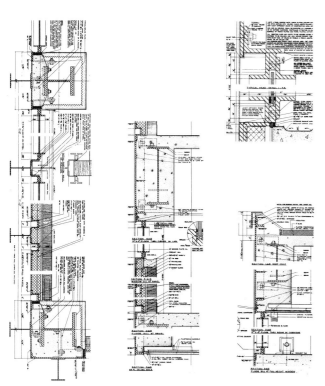

81–82. Highfield House Apartments, Baltimore: 1963–5.

91. 860/880 Lake Shore Drive Apartments.

92. The Science Center, Duquesne University.

87–90. The Science Center, Duquesne University, Pittsburgh: 1962–8.

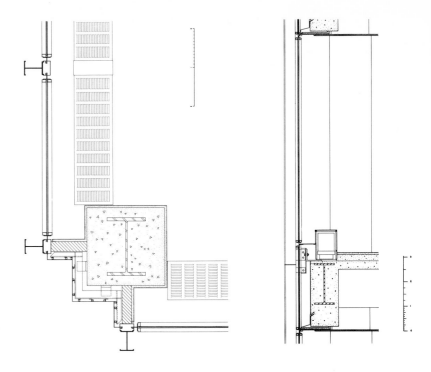

93–94. Seagram Building, New York: 1954–8.

(3) In this solution the skin is located in front of the structure and, except for supporting connections, is independent of it. The structure is within the building's ambient temperature field and consequently the expansion and contraction problems mentioned above do not apply. When asked whether he had a preference for this or the 860 type of skin solution, Mies van der Rohe answered that either was possible, but he considered the former a more technological solution.

An example of where this method was applied to a steel-framed building may be seen at the Seagram Building in New York, 1954–8, where the skin consists of bronze mullions, column covers, spandrel panels, glazing frames and louvres; and bronze tinted plate glass. Assembly: the skin was assembled in separate elements, i.e. mullions in one-storey high lengths, window and spandrel subframe, spandrel plate, glass and glazing frames (page 61).

Another application of this skin solution to a steel-framed building may be seen at the Toronto-Dominion Centre in Canada, 1963–9. Here the skin consists of steel mullions, floor fascia plates and column covers—painted matte black; aluminium glazing frames—with a black baked-on finish, and bronze-grey tinted glass. Assembly; initially the skin was assembled on the building in separate pieces, but when this method proved to have a number of disadvantages, it was replaced by the fabrication on the site of two-storey, 30 ft and 40 ft wide units, which were then hoisted up into position (page 65).

An example where the skin is located in front of a reinforced concrete flat slab structure may be seen at the Commonwealth Promenade Apartments in Chicago, 1953–6. Here the skin comprises aluminium mullions, floor and roof spandrels, column covers and glazing frames; with grey-tinted glass. Assembly: the skin was shop fabricated in one-storey, 21 ft wide units (page 57).

Another application of this skin solution to a reinforced concrete flat slab structure may be seen at the Colonnade Park Apartments in Newark, 1958–60. Here the skin consists of aluminium mullions, floor and roof spandrels, glazing frames and under-window screens, with grey-tinted glass. The cast aluminium under-window screens protect a recessed and continuous perimeter housing for individual air-conditioning units and also permits the natural ventilation of the apartments. Assembly: the skin was assembled from separate man-handleable pieces from the building's interior (page 59).

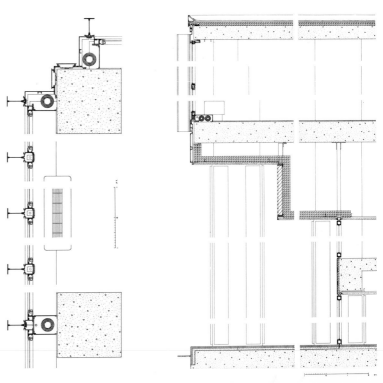

102–103. Commonwealth Promenade Apartments, Chicago: 1953–6.

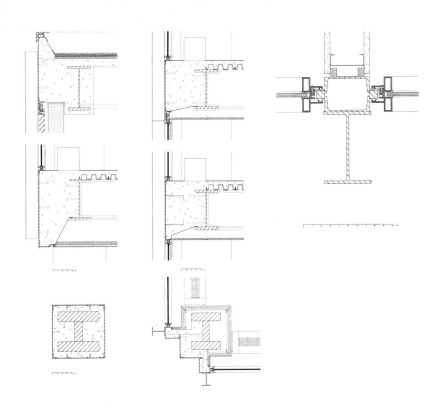

95–99. Toronto Dominion Bank Tower, Toronto: 1963–7.

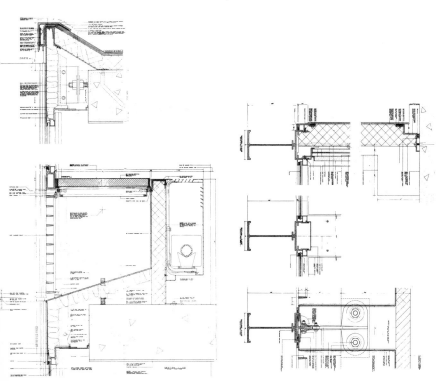

104–106. Colonnade Apartments, Newark: 1958–60.

100. Seagram Building.

107. Commonwealth Promenade Apartments.

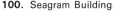

101. Toronto Dominion Bank Tower.

108. Colonnade Apartments.

HIGH-RISE BUILDINGS: SCALE

The conviction that one building element should relate to another—through an organic progression ranging from the smallest to the largest—brought about the very logical scale breakdown systems which Mies van der Rohe's buildings possess. From a building's total mass the initial scale reduction is set by the structural frame. The structural frame (which is determined by the building's function) may be fully expressed by bringing both the floor beam/spandrels and the columns to the exterior face—as is the case with the Promontary Apartments and 860 Lake Shore Drive; or it may be partially expressed externally by the floor spandrels only—as is the case with the Seagram Building and the Toronto-Dominion Centre. At the base of the building, the structural frame stands free of enclosing elements and the high and open ground floors provide a point of transition between the scale of the exterior whole and that of the office or apartment spaces of the interior.

A further scale reduction is made on the typical office or apartment floors by the subdivision of each structural bay into a number of equal parts relative to the building's module and by the expression of these parts through the use of projecting mullions. The module, as has already been noted, relates directly to the interior activities; by its visual expression as a mullion, a common and recognizable element is introduced which connects the interior with the exterior and unifies the whole.

These organic scale graduations clarify the magnitude of a building, ease the gap between human scale and building scale, and help to define the spaces between the buildings. This latter aspect is discussed in the section of this book which deals with Mies van der Rohe's urban spaces (page 113).

109. 860/880 Lake Shore Drive Apartments, Chicago: 1948–51. View looking towards Lake Michigan.

110. Toronto Dominion Bank Tower, Toronto: 1963–7. Plaza entrance.   ▷

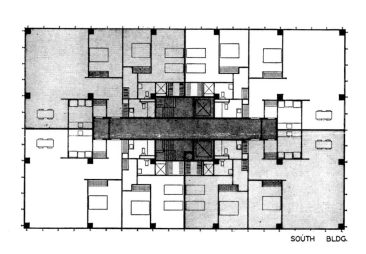

NORTH BLDG.

The ideas underlying Mies van der Rohe's glass skyscraper projects of the 1920's reached their first practical realization in 1951 with the construction of two steel and glass apartment towers on Lake Shore Drive in Chicago. Mies van der Rohe's first high-rise apartment buildings—Promontory Apartments of 1946–9 and the projected Algonquin Apartments of 1948—had utilized reinforced concrete frame construction; for the 860/880 Lake Shore Drive project, he decided to use steel construction because the application of reinforced concrete to very tall buildings was still in the development stage at that time.

Available financing, rather than the permissible floor area ratio, determined the project's total floor area; and this area was accommodated in two buildings in order that full advantage could be taken of the site's magnificent location. Limitations of population and height were set by: (1) Elevatoring—an extra elevator would have been required if more apartment floors had been added above the present 26 stories; (2) Smoke shaft—the city building code would have required the introduction of a smoke shaft adjacent to one of the fire stairs had the buildings exceeded their present height.

Both towers are three by five 21 ft bays on plan. 860—the south tower—was originally laid out with four three-bedroom apartments on each floor, while 880—the north tower—had eight one-bedroom apartments on each floor. In many cases, the plan of a particular floor was modified, or has been so subsequently, as the space requirements of the co-operative owners have changed over the years, a fact that attests to the flexibility of the planning concept (as described on page 37). 860 Lake Shore Drive is discussed from the city planning view-point on page 119.

SOUTH BLDG.

◁ 111. 860/880 Lake Shore Drive Apartments: 1948–51. Night view.

◁ 112. 860/880 Lake Shore Drive Apartments. Daytime view.

113. 860/880 Lake Shore Drive Apartments. Typical apartment floor plans as shown in the rental booklet.

114. 860/880. Apartment interior—living room.

115. 860/880. Apartment interior—living room.

116. 860/880. Apartment interior—bedroom.

117. 860/880. Entrance lobby. Furniture: Barcelona table and chairs.   ▷

860 and 880 Lake Shore Drive Apartments

Building module.	5 ft 3 in
Structural bay.	21 ft square
Overall thickness of typical floor	1 ft $7\frac{1}{2}$ in
Clear height of typical floor.	8 ft $4\frac{1}{2}$ in
Clear height of ground floor.	17 ft 1 in
Number of floors above grade	26
Number of floors below grade	2
Height of building.	270 ft
Overall dimensions of plan	64 ft 10 in × 106 ft 10 in
Gross area per floor.	6930 sq ft
Ratio of core to gross area*.	8.2%
Gross area of each building above grade	180,000 sq ft
Total number of apartments.	860:96 880: 192

* Core: elevator and mechanical shafts, fire stairs.

Structure and materials. The buildings have fireproofed steel structural frames and are enclosed by skins consisting of welded steel components, aluminium glazing frames and clear plate glass (skin details page 46). All exposed steel is painted matte black. On the ground floors the soffits are of cement plaster painted white, translucent glass is used around the service areas, and travertine is used for facing the cores and paving the lobby floors and terrace areas. To preserve a degree of neutrality from the buildings' exterior, all apartments are provided with light-grey drapery linings.

Site data on the 860 and 880 Lake Shore Drive Apartments is listed on page 119.

118. Commonwealth Promenade Apartments, Chicago: 1953–6. Ground level view.

119. Commonwealth Promenade Apartments. Air view.

120. Commonwealth Promenade Apartments. View from Lincoln Park.

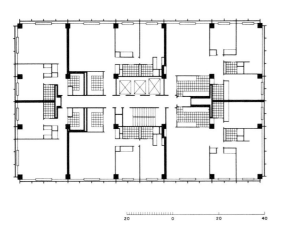

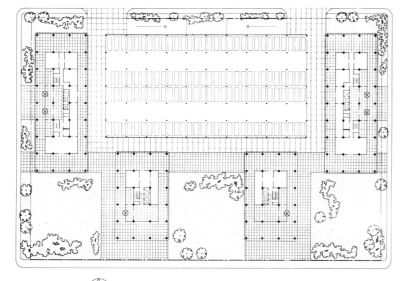

COMMONWEALTH PROMENADE APARTMENTS: 1953–6

The initial project for Commonwealth Promenade Apartments in Chicago consisted of four 27-storey apartment buildings accommodating a total of 750 units with a low garage structure located in between. Unfortunately, due to the death of Herbert Greenwald, the developer (page 177), only the southern pair of buildings were completed. These employed structural and skin solutions which were more economical than those used at 860 Lake Shore Drive (it was possible to accommodate an extra floor in the same height because of the shallower floor construction), and they consequently became archetypes for Mies van der Rohe's subsequent apartment buildings.

Area of site	1.57 acres
Permissible floor area ratio	8
Proportion of site occupied by apartment buildings	27.5%
Gross area above grade (including parking building)	534,500 sq ft
Gross area below grade	67,200 sq ft
Total number of apartments	375
Population/density (people per acre)	1143/728
Covered car parking	223 cars
Building module	5 ft 3 in
Structural bay	21 ft square
Overall thickness of typical floor (varies from)	9 in to 12 in
Clear height of typical floor	8 ft
Clear height of ground floor	16 ft $4\frac{1}{2}$ in
Number of floors above grade	27
Number of floors below grade	1
Height of buildings	253 ft
Overall dimensions of plan—north building	67 ft × 109 ft
Overall dimensions of plan—south building	67 ft × 172 ft
Gross area per floor—north building	7290 sq ft
Gross area per floor—south building	11,510 sq ft
Ratio of core* to gross area—north building	4.6%
Ratio of core* to gross area—south building	4.2%

* Core: elevator and mechanical shafts, fire stairs.

Structure and materials. The buildings are of reinforced flat slab construction (the tallest at the time to be so constructed) and are enclosed by skins consisting of natural colour aluminium components and grey-tinted glass (skin details page 49). On the ground floors the soffits are of cement plaster painted white, translucent glass is used around the service areas, the cores are faced with verde antique marble, and the lobby floors and terraces are paved with terrazzo.

121. Commonwealth Promenade Apartments. Plan of typical apartment floor of 8-bay building.

122. Commonwealth Promenade Apartments. Plan of typical apartment floor of 5-bay building.

123. Commonwealth Promenade Apartments. Site plan.

COLONNADE PARK REDEVELOPMENT: 1958–60

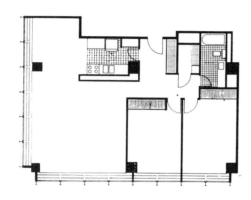

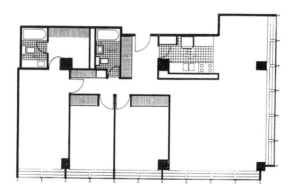

During the 1950's, the City of Newark, New Jersey embarked upon an extensive building programme in which private developers were invited to redevelop the city's condemned sites. To encourage this type of action, the Federal Housing Agency insured bank loans on the basis of certain minimum planning standards and relative rental scales. Colonnade Park was the first scheme to be built under Newark's redevelopment programme. Colonnade Apartments, the building illustrated here, accommodates 560 units and is located on the western of the two sites which form the development. In this building, half of the tenants face directly upon an adjacement public park, while the other half have the Manhattan skyline as their fourth wall.

Area of site	6.7 acres
Permissible number of dwelling units per acre	85
Proportion of site occupied by building/s	10%
Gross area above grade	617,000 sq ft
Gross area below grade	27,000 sq ft
Total number of apartments	560
Population/density (people per acre)	1200/180
Building module	5 ft
Structural bay	20 ft square
Overall thickness of typical floor	9 in
Clear height of typical floor	8 ft
Clear height of ground floor	15 ft 6 in
Number of floors above grade	21
Number of floors below grade	1
Height of building	195 ft
Overall dimensions of plan	66 ft × 446 ft
Gross area per floor	29,410 sq ft
Ratio of core to gross area*	3.8%

* Core: elevator and mechanical shafts, fire stairs.

Structure and materials. This building is of light-weight reinforced concrete flat slab construction and is enclosed by a skin consisting of natural colour aluminium components which incorporate a housing for individual air-conditioning units, the skin is glazed with grey-tinted glass (skin details page 49). On the ground floor the soffit is of cement plaster painted white, the elevator cores are faced with travertine and the stair cores with buff-coloured brick, the lobby floors are paved with terrazzo and the terrace with concrete.

◁ **124.** Colonnade Apartments, Newark: 1958–60. View from Branchbrook Park.

125–128. Colonnade Apartments. Typical apartment plans.

129. Colonnade Apartments. Typical apartment floor plan.

Waynesburg College Library
Waynesburg, Pa. 15370

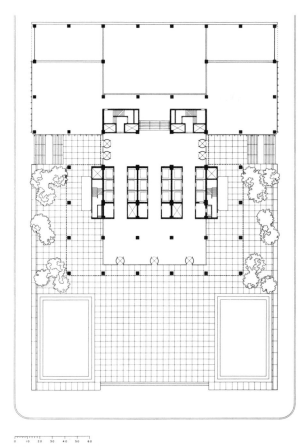

THE SEAGRAM BUILDING: 1954–8

The concept of the glass skyscraper as envisioned by Mies van der Rohe in his projects of the 1920's had been a stimulus to many architects, but it was not, however, until the 1950's—when he built a series of high-rise apartment buildings—that Mies van der Rohe also had the opportunity of realizing the practical possibilities of these early concepts. The commission for the Seagram Building, in which he was to be joined by Philip Johnson as co-architect and Phyllis Lambert as director of planning (page 178), enabled him to further this development on a scale and in a manner that had not been previously available to him.

Samuel Bronfman, Chairman of the Board of Joseph Seagram and Sons, had decided to construct a building of fine quality to house the company's head office together with additional space for leaseholders —the latter in units as small as 500 sq ft if this should be necessary. The square footage to be built was determined by combining the area needed by the Seagram company with the figure that the real estate consultants considered marketable to leaseholders. Although the total arrived at by this method was well below that which would have been permissible by code, it was decided that in view of the type of occupancy envisaged there would be no economic advantage to be gained from filling the space envelope. The Seagram Building has, furthermore, shown that an additional investment in the fabric of a building is capable of securing very considerable returns in rental, both initially and at the times of rent reassessment. (Other factors which influenced the design of the Seagram Building are discussed on page 127 where the city planning aspects of the project are considered.)

'My approach to the Seagram Building was no different from that of any other building that I might build,' Mies van der Rohe recalled. 'My idea, or better "direction", in which I go is toward a clear structure and construction—this applies not to any one problem but to all architectural problems which I approach. I am, in fact, completely opposed to the idea that a specific building should have an individual character. Rather, I believe that it should express a universal character which has been determined by the total problem which archi-

◁ **130.** Seagram Building, New York: 1954–8. Night-time view.

◁ **131.** Seagram Building. Day-time view.

132. Seagram Building. Plan of typical office floor in tower.

133. Seagram Building. Plaza level plan.

tecture must strive to solve. On the Seagram Building, since it was to be built in New York and since it was to be the first major office building which I was to build, I asked for two types of advice for the development of the plans. One, the best real estate advice as to the types of desirable rentable space and, two, professional advice regarding the New York Building Code. With my direction established and with these advisers, it was then only a matter of hard work.'

The great success of the Seagram Building brought Mies van der Rohe—then in his seventy-second year—wider recognition and many important new commissions. The work undertaken during his last ten years was, with few exceptions, on a scale comparable to that of the Seagram project and, in the case of the multi-building urban centres which he built in Chicago, Montreal and Toronto, directly related to it.

Building module	4 ft 7½ in
Structural bay	27 ft 9 in square
Overall thickness of typical floor	3 ft 1½ in
Clear height of typical floor	8 ft 10½ in
Clear height of ground floor	23 ft 10 in
Number of floors above grade	39
Number of floors below grade	2½
Height of building	516 ft
Overall dimensions of plan (tower)	87 ft 7 in × 143 ft 1 in
(spine)	27 ft 9 in × 87 ft 7 in
Gross area per floor—2nd to 4th floors	31,955 sq ft
Gross area per floor—5th to 10th floors	22,225 sq ft
Gross area per floor—above 10th floor (tower)	14,933 sq ft
Ratio of core to gross area—2nd to 4th floors*	20.4%
Ratio of core to gross area—5th to 10th floors*	26.2%
Ratio of core to gross area—above 10th floor*	27.3%
Gross area of building above grade	694,000 sq ft
Gross area of building below grade	157,000 sq ft
Underground car parking	130 cars

* Core: total area occupied by passenger and service elevator shafts and lobbies, mechanical ducts, telephone and electric rooms, toilets, fire stairs.

Structure and materials. This building has a fireproofed steel structural frame and is enclosed by a skin consisting of bronze components and bronze-tinted glass (skin details page 48). On the ground floor the soffit is of pinkish-grey glass mosaic, the cores are faced with travertine, and the lobby floor and plaza areas are paved with pinkish-grey granite.

Site data on the Seagram Building is listed on page 127.

134. Seagram Building. Reception area of Seagram executive offices.

135. Seagram Building. Interior of a Seagram executive office.

136. Seagram Building. Plaza entrance lobby interior.

137. Seagram Building. View of plaza from Park Avenue. ▷

◁ **138.** Toronto-Dominion Centre: 1963–9. Aerial view during construction.

139. Toronto Dominion Bank Tower. Toronto Dominion Bank board room, 54th floor.

140. Toronto Dominion Bank Tower. Entrance to tower from Wellington Street.

141. Toronto Dominion Bank Tower. Toronto Dominion Bank Executive Suite, 54th floor.

142. Toronto Dominion Bank Tower. Typical office floor during construction.

TORONTO DOMINION BANK TOWER: 1963-7

Toronto-Dominion Centre, of which this 56-storey office tower is one element, was undertaken as a joint venture in which Mies van der Rohe was consultant to the Canadian architectural firms of John B. Parkin Associates and Bregman and Hamann. The Toronto Dominion Bank Tower provides over 1.3 million square feet net for multiple tenancy occupancy; the range of leased space extending from tenants who occupy one or more full floors, to some with areas as small as 360 sq ft (two modules). Elevatoring is divided into four rises, with cross-over facilities linking one rise to the next. The structural bay of 30 ft by 40 ft proved to offer individual tenants great flexibility in the planning of their spaces. (The Centre's management assessed the absence of free-standing columns in the office spaces as providing a 15% saving in office area and a 5% increase in employee efficiency—a total rental saving of over $2.00 sq ft.) Toronto-Dominion Centre as a whole is discussed, with particular emphasis to its city planning aspects, on page 137.

Building module	5 ft
Structural bay	30 ft $\times$ 40 ft
Overall thickness of typical floor	3 ft
Clear height of typical floor	9 ft
Clear height of ground floor	26 ft
Number of floors above grade	56
Number of floors below grade	3
Height of building	731 ft
Overal dimensions of plan	124 ft 3 in $\times$ 244 ft 3 in
Gross area per floor	30,250 sq ft
Ratio of core to gross area—low-rise floors*	22.7%
Ratio of core to gross area—high-rise floors*	14.7%
Gross area of building above grade	1,686,875 sq ft

* Core: total area occupied by passenger and service elevator shafts and lobbies, mechanical ducts, telephone and electric rooms, toilets, fire stairs.

Structure and materials. This building has a fireproofed steel structural frame and is enclosed by a skin consisting of welded steel components, black aluminium louvres and glazing frames, and bronze grey-tinted glass (skin details page 49). All exposed steel is painted matte black. On the ground floor, the soffit is of grey glass mosaic, the cores are faced with travertine, and the lobby floor and plaza areas are paved with St. John's grey granite.

Further data on the Toronto-Dominion Centre is listed on page 138.

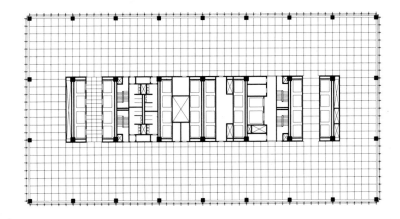

143. Toronto Dominion Bank Tower. Typical low-rise office floor plan.

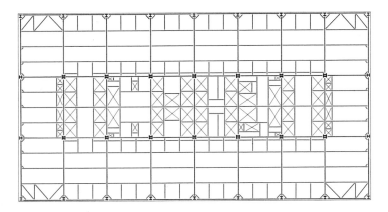

144. Toronto Dominion Bank Tower. Steel framing plan of typical low-rise office floor.

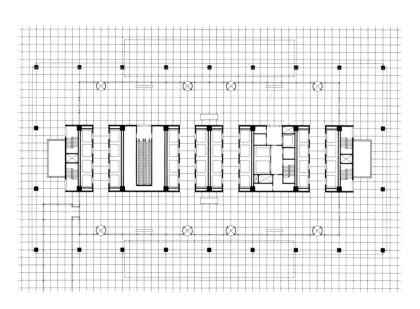

0   30   60   90 FT

145. Toronto Dominion Bank Tower. Plaza level plan.

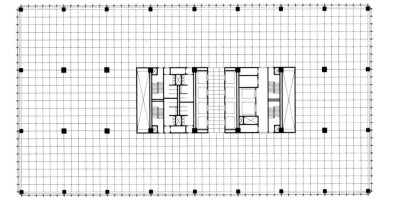

146. Toronto Dominion Bank Tower. Typical high-rise office floor plan.

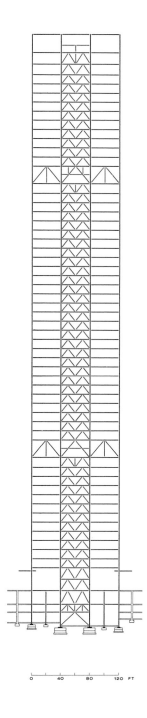

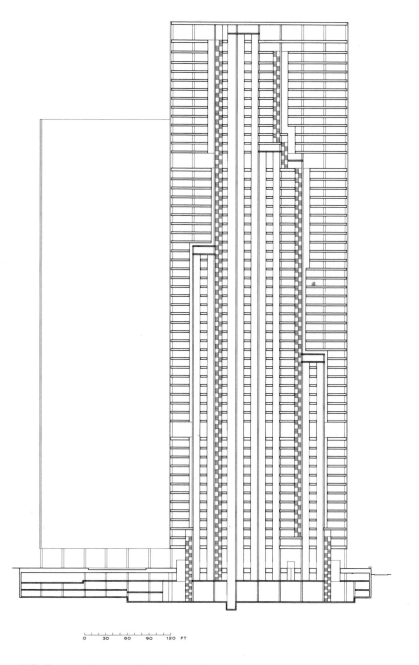

147. Toronto Dominion Bank Tower. Section through tower showing steel structure.

148. Toronto Dominion Bank Tower. Section through tower showing stairs and elevators.

149. U.S. Courthouse and Federal Office Building, Chicago: 1959–64. View from the west.

150. U.S. Courthouse and Federal Office Building. Detail view from the east.

151. U.S. Courthouse and Federal Office Building. Typical courtroom.

152. U.S. Courthouse and Federal Office Building. Typical courtroom.

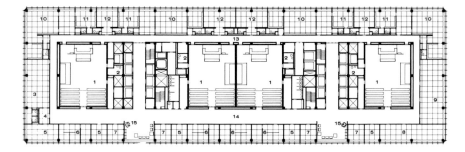

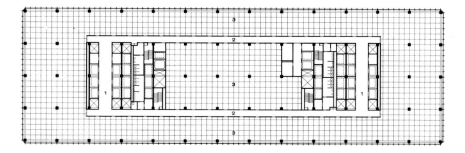

153. U.S. Courthouse and Federal Office Building. Typical courts floor plan.

154. U.S. Courthouse and Federal Office Building. Typical office floor plan.

155. U.S. Courthouse and Federal Office Building. Ground floor plan.

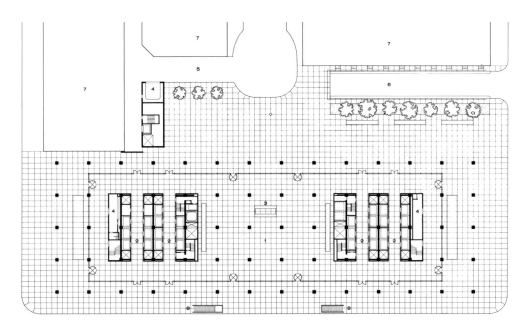

U.S. COURTHOUSE AND FEDERAL OFFICE BUILDING: 1959–64.

This building comprises one element of the United States Government's Federal Center complex in Chicago (page 133), a joint venture in which Mies van der Rohe associated with the Chicago architectural firms of: Schmidt, Garden & Erikson; C. F. Murphy Associates; and A. Epstein & Sons, Inc. The building illustrates a solution to the problem of accommodating a number of large-scale spaces (courtrooms) within the structure of a typical office building.

The first stage of the Chicago Federal Center's programme called for 21 courtrooms, together with their related activities, and general purpose office space for various government agencies. The decision to accommodate both functions in a single 30-storey building on that portion of the site which lay to the east of Dearborn Street was made in order that the courts might continue to operate—until their transfer to the new building—in the existing Federal Building located on the adjacent block to the west of Dearborn Street.

The courthouse functions are located on the twelve upper floors of the U.S. Courthouse and Federal Office building, where the absence of low-rise elevator banks releases centrally located area for such large-scale functions. The two-storey-high courtrooms are, therefore, planned within the two central bays of the four-bay-deep building; the outer bay to the east accommodates the judges' chambers, while that to the west houses court related public activities. At street level, the high and open ground floor is devoted entirely to entrance functions. The large space which occurs between the two groups of elevator cores, and which is visible from both major faces of the building, is occupied by public seating areas, a government information centre and exhibition space.

Building module	4 ft 8 in
Structural bay	28 ft square
Overall thickness of typical floor	3 ft
Clear height of typical floor	9 ft
Clear height of ground floor	26 ft
Number of floors above grade	30
Number of floors below grade	$2\frac{1}{2}$
Height of building	383 ft
Overall dimensions of plan	116 ft 4 in × 368 ft 4 in
Gross area per floor	42,830 sq ft
Ratio of core to gross area*	20%
Gross area of building above grade	1,285,000 sq ft

*Core: total area occupied by passenger and service elevator shafts and lobbies, mechanical ducts, telephone and electric rooms, toilets, fire stairs.

Structure and materials. This building has a fireproofed steel structural frame and is enclosed by a skin consisting of welded steel components, bronze-grey colour aluminium louvres and glazing frames, and bronze-grey tinted glass. All exposed steel is painted matte black. On the ground floor the soffit is of cement plaster painted white, and Rockville granite is used to face the cores and to pave the lobby floor and plaza areas. Further data on the Chicago Federal Center is listed on page 133.

Low-rise Skeleton Frame Buildings

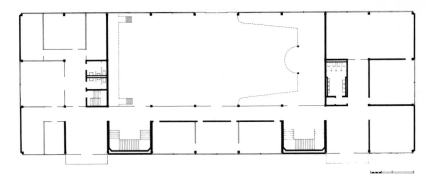

156. Alumni Memorial Hall, Illinois Institute of Technology, Chicago: 1945–6. Plan.

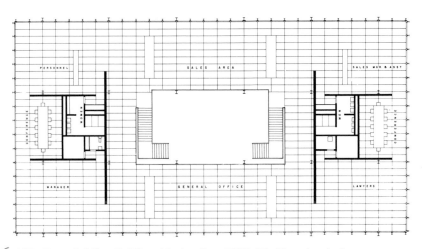

157. Bacardi Office Building, Mexico City: 1957–61. Plan of main floor.

158. Bacardi Office Building, Mexico City. Plan of ground floor.

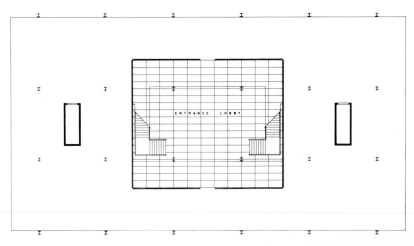

For both low- and high-rise building types, the structural bay establishes a regular frame within which the needs of similar and dissimilar functions may be accommodated with optimum ease and possible future change. In the low-rise building, however, there is usually far more freedom in determining the structural bay; limitations which result from multiple vertical repetition and accumulative weight being absent, greater spans may be economically feasible and—because of the different type of occupancy—functionally desirable. Such conditions can produce a more varied spatial character and an altogether looser plan assembly than is possible for high-rise structures.

In Mies van der Rohe's low-rise skeleton frame buildings, accommodation which needs natural light is planned at the periphery. The interior areas, free of the high-rise building's extensive elevator and mechanical service cores, are opened up as much as possible to form circulation spaces around free-standing auditoria and other functions for which natural light is not essential. The enclosed character of these interior spaces is often relieved by the introduction of garden courts which provide visual and physical contact with the outside and bring nature into the heart of a building. The wide range of spatial possibilities inherent in the low-rise skeleton frame building may be appreciated from the three examples which follow.

159. Alumni Memorial Hall. Exterior view.

160. Alumni Memorial Hall. Interior corridor.

161. Alumni Memorial Hall. Interior stair.

162. Bacardi Office Building, Mexico City. Exterior view.

163. Bacardi Office Building, Mexico City. Interior view of main floor.

164. Alumni Hall wall detail (Metallurgical and Chemical Engineering Building utilized aluminium glazing frames).

165. Alumni Hall exterior corner detail (Metallurgical and Chemical Engineering Building similar).

◁ **166.** Metallurgical and Chemical Engineering Building, Illinois Institute of Technology, Chicago: 1945–6. Exterior view.

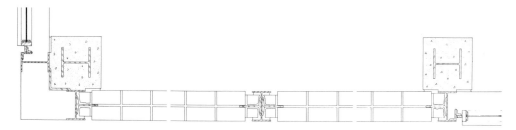

167. Alumni Hall exterior wall details (Metallurgical and Chemical Engineering Building utilized aluminium glazing frames).

168. Metallurgical and Chemical Engineering Building, I.I.T. Plan of ground floor.

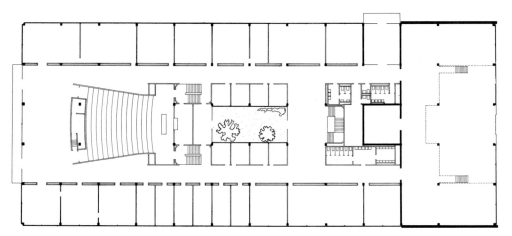

METALLURGICAL AND CHEMICAL ENGINEERING BUILDING AT I.I.T.: 1945–6

The two-storey Metallurgical and Chemical Engineering Building illustrates a typical application of the 24 ft square module upon which Mies van der Rohe based his Master Plan of Illinois Institute of Technology campus (page 115). The building is five bays in width by twelve in length (the 36 ft bay at one end is combined with its adjacent 24 ft bay to form a double height workshop/laboratory). In the long direction the outer bays accommodate classrooms and laboratories, while the three bays in between are opened up to form broad entrance and circulation spaces for the free-standing auditorium, administrative offices and toilet block. An interior garden court provides outside contact for the offices, conference rooms and the circulation space.

Building module	12 ft
Structural bay	24 ft square
Structural bays at north end of building	24 ft×36 ft
Overall thickness of floor	1 ft 7 in
Clear height of typical floor	11 ft 11 in
Number of floors above grade	2
Number of floors below grade	1
Height of building	28 ft 6 in
Overall dimensions of plan	122 ft 7 in×303 ft 7 in
Gross area per floor	36,000 sq ft
Gross area above grade	72,000 sq ft
Gross area below grade	36,000 sq ft
Area of garden court	1,150 sq ft

Structure and materials. This building is typical of those which Mies van der Rohe designed for the I.I.T. campus. It has a fireproofed steel structural frame and is enclosed by a skin consisting of welded steel components, aluminium sash, clear plate glass and solid panels of buff-coloured brick. All exposed steel is painted matt black. The skin is attached to the exterior face of the fireproofed steel skeleton; the corners at the south end of the building are turned by terminating the skin on the centre line of the corner column—the portion of the column which is thereby exposed acting as the pivoting agent (this solution is similar to that used for the earlier Alumni Memorial Hall). At the north end of the building, this solution is modified in order to accommodate the needs of the two-storey-high workshop. In the interior the ceilings are of plaster with panels of acoustic tile, the floors are paved with a dark grey and white flecked terrazzo—and in some areas with resilient tile, the partitions are plastered and painted off-white, and doors and door frames and the south wall panelling of the auditorium are of oak.

169. Commons Building, Illinois Institute of Technology: 1952–3. Exterior view from the east.

170. Commons Building, I.I.T. Interior view of central space.

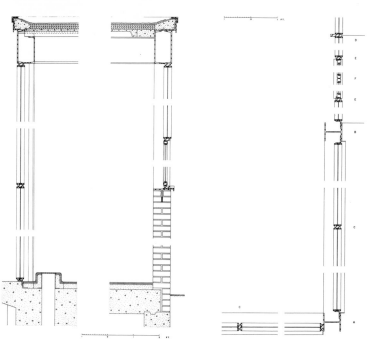

171. Commons Building, I.I.T. Detail sections through exterior wall.

172. Commons Building, I.I.T. Plan through exterior wall.

173. Commons Building, I.I.T. Plan at ground level.

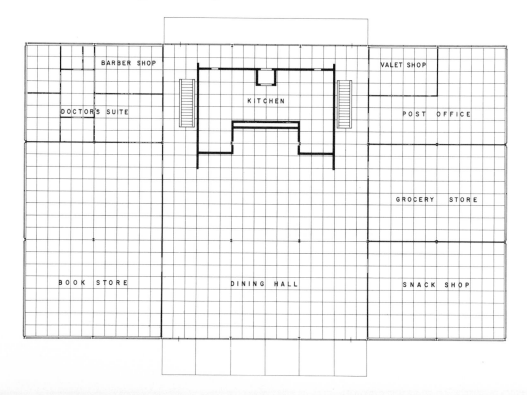

THE COMMONS AT I.I.T.: 1952–3

The Commons building at Illinois Institute of Technology functions as a town centre for the campus. It accommodates dining, meeting and lounge facilities, supplemented by such functions as a post office, a doctor's office, laundry and shops of various types.

The fact that the Chicago building code allowed the steel skeleton to remain un-fireproofed permitted its form and welded assembly to be freely displayed. This in turn solicited a direct and unaffected approach to both structure and detailing—observe, for example, the manner in which roof deck, beam and girder are brought together at the column head.

The central three bays of this seven bay wide structure form an open hall extending from the front to the rear of the building. The entrance doors open directly into this hall, and from it access is gained to all of the perimeter spaces. This division of the plan into perimeter screened spaces and interior open space—with a single free-standing core—is somewhat similar in concept to that of I.I.T.'s Metallurgical and Chemical Engineering Building. The perimeter spaces of The Commons building, however, are treated more openly in relation to the interior space, and because of this the full interior volume of the building becomes revealed; while at the same time making it possible for sky and trees to be seen from any point on the plan.

Building module	4 ft
Structural bay	24 ft × 32 ft
Overal dimensions of plan	97 ft × 168 ft
Gross area per floor	16,800 sq ft
Clear height of main floor	16 ft
Clear height of lower floor	9 ft 4 in
Height of building	17 ft 9 in

Structure and materials. This building has an un-fireproofed and exposed steel structural frame set above a reinforced concrete sub-structure. The skin consists of steel framing members, with solid panels of buff-coloured brick, and glazed areas of clear plate glass. All exposed steel is painted matte black. Interior partitions consist of obscured glass or exposed concrete block up to door height with clear plate glass above; the kitchen core walls are plastered and painted, and the floors are paved with a dark grey and white flecked terrazzo.

LIBRARY AND ADMINISTRATION BUILDING: 1944

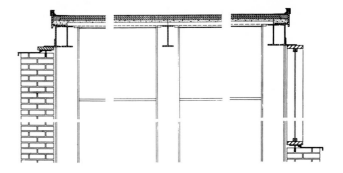

While there is little point in regretting the fact that many interesting projects do not reach the stage of final realization, in the case of Mies van der Rohe's I.I.T. Library and Administration Building and his Chicago Convention Hall (page 101)—buildings to which he was particularly attached—this constitutes a considerable deprivation to architecture. These two projects represented general solutions to new problems, and had they been built, they would undoubtedly have made important contributions.

The Library and Administration Building was essentially a single 192 ft wide, 312 ft long and 24 ft high space. Although the building was of the low-rise skeleton framed type, by the use of low partitions, free-standing cores, a floating mezzanine and a garden court, Mies van der Rohe was able to provide local screening between the functions, while at the same time preserving a feeling for the total volume of the building. The magnitudes of the individual functions and the magnitude of the building as a whole were to be sensed as parallel experiences aimed towards the creation of a single space.

Building module.	12 ft × 12 ft 9½ in
Structural bay.	24 ft × 64 ft
Overall dimensions of plan	192 ft × 312 ft
Gross area of main floor (including book stack).	55,300 sq ft
Gross area of mezzanine	17,800 sq ft
Area of garden court	4600 sq ft
Area below grade (book stack)	4600 sq ft
Clear height of main floor.	24 ft 8 in
Clear height under mezzanine.	12 ft 6 in
Height of building.	28 ft 6 in

Structure and materials. This building has an un-fireproofed and exposed steel structural frame. The skin consists of steel framing members with solid panels of buff-coloured brick and glazed areas of clear plate glass. All exposed steel is painted matte black.

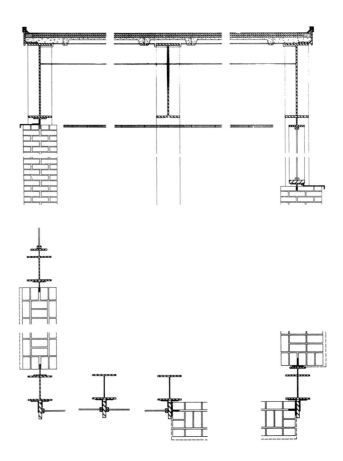

174. Library and Administration Building, Illinois Institute of Technology, Chicago: Project: 1944. Exterior wall details: above —section; below—plan.

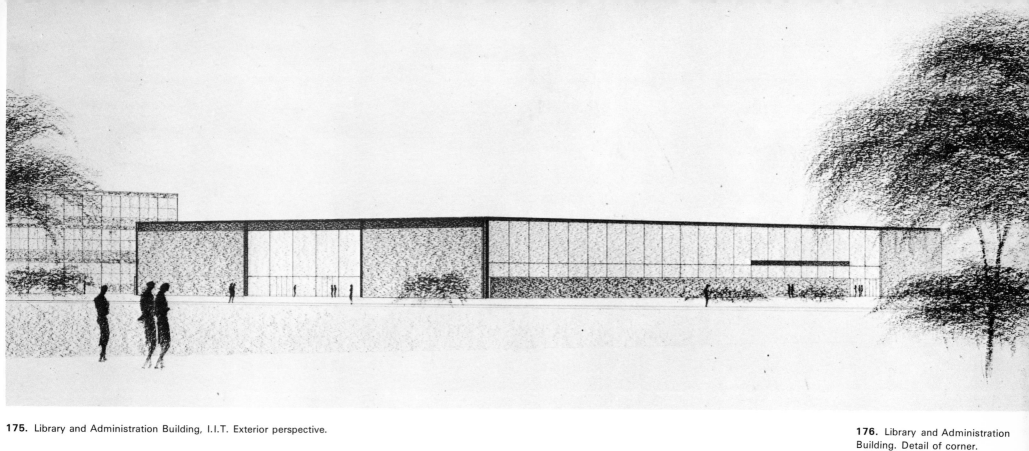

175. Library and Administration Building, I.I.T. Exterior perspective.

176. Library and Administration Building. Detail of corner.

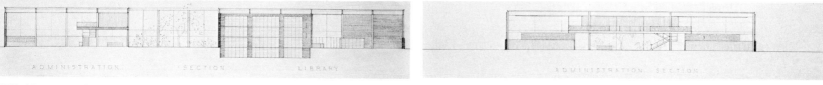

177. Library and Administration Building, I.I.T. Long section.

179. Library and Administration Building, I.I.T. Main floor plan.

178. Library and Administration Building, I.I.T. Cross section.

180. Library and Administration Building, I.I.T. Mezzanine floor plan.

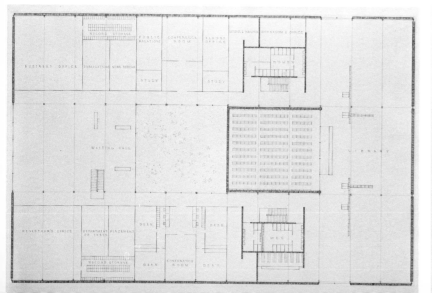

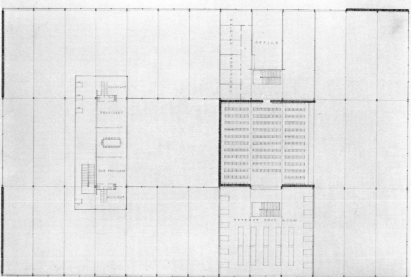

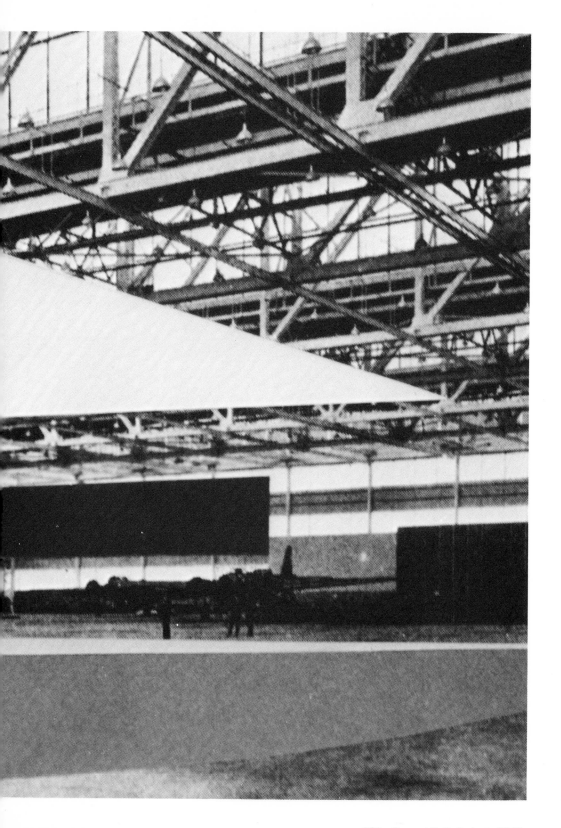

Clear Span Buildings

Almost concurrently with his work on the Library and Administration Building, Mies van der Rohe was working on a project in which he had placed a number of free planes under a peripherally supported roof structure. For this study he chose to use a photograph of Albert Kahn and Associates' Glen Martin Aircraft Assembly Building at Baltimore—one of the largest clear span enclosed buildings then in existence.

Although this project was made specifically for a concert hall, implicit in its conception was the possibility of accommodating almost any function relative to the magnitude of the structure. The building provided a single column free space where optimum flexibility in the placing of functional elements was possible—it was, in fact, a form of universal space.

In the course of applying the clear span concept to buildings of differing functions and magnitudes, Mies van der Rohe discovered that one or more related activities may be brought together and unified within a single space. A possibility which has the advantage of a built-in provision for change, precisely because the structural shell is independent of the functional subdivisions.

In these buildings the subsidiary functions for which enclosure is essential—such as toilets, storage areas and mechanical rooms, together with those back-up activities which operate independently of the major space—are accommodated either in free-standing cores on the main floor, or on a separate level directly below. Rainwater pipes, air-conditioning and electrical services are brought up through free-standing and non-structural duct shafts for horizontal distribution within the roof structure when its depth permits this, and when not, above a suspended ceiling.

Air-conditioning of the clear span spaces is accomplished by peripheral floor supply outlets working in conjunction with ceiling outlets; return air being extracted through openings in the free-standing service stacks.

Unlike the column-free spaces of the past (which generally accommodated the needs of one function and were spatially singular in character), those of Mies van der Rohe's clear span buildings have been given an entirely different meaning through his introduction of freely disposed elements of a non-structural nature. In these buildings the primary structure (the enclosing shell) is clearly expressed and separated from the secondary structure (the space-defining elements). We experience, at one and the same time, the relationship between the plurality of the particular spaces and the singularity of the total space—with all the rich variations of scale and space

181. Concert Hall. Project: 1942.

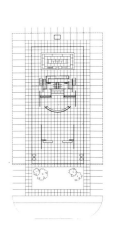

182. German Pavilion, International Exposition, Barcelona: 1928–9. Interior view.

183. Crown Hall, Illinois Institute of Technology, Chicago: 1950–6. Night-time view.

184. Crown Hall, I.I.T.

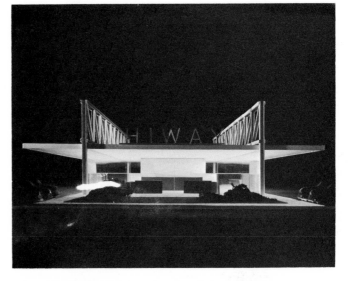

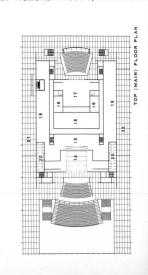

185. Fifty foot by fifty foot house. Project: 1950–1.

186. Fifty foot by fifty foot house.

187. Cantor Drive-in Restaurant, Indianapolis. Project: 1945–6.

188. Cantor Drive-in Restaurant.

189. Farnsworth House, Plano: 1945–50.

190. Farnsworth House. Plan.

191. National Theatre, Mannheim. Project: 1952–3.

192. National Theatre, Mannheim.

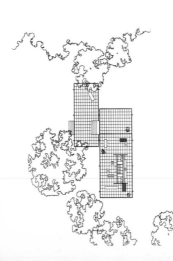

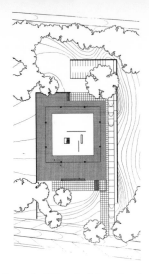

193. Bacardi Office Building, Santiago de Cuba. Project: 1957.

194. Bacardi Office Building, Santiago de Cuba.

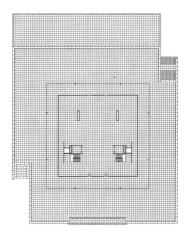

195. New National Gallery, Berlin: 1962–8. Aerial view.

196. New National Gallery, Berlin.

197. Convention Hall, Chicago. Project: 1953–4.

198. Convention Hall. Plan.

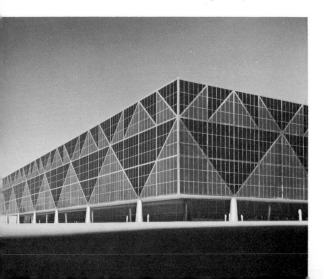

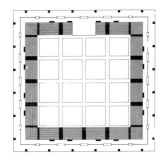

that this engenders. The development from the separation of structural and space elements at Barcelona, through the multi-function space of the Library and Administration Building, to the eventual removal of interior supports entirely had followed a logical course and was typical of Mies van der Rohe's way of work.

Mies van der Rohe's clear span buildings may be grouped into three categories of differing structural type and progressively increasing magnitude:

(1) Those buildings having a rectangular roof plane supported between perimeter columns in the manner of the Farnsworth House (28 ft × 77 ft).

(2) Those buildings having a rectangular roof plane attached to the underside of exposed trusses or bents as is the case with Crown Hall (120 ft × 220 ft); the Drive-in Restaurant (105 ft × 150 ft); and the Mannheim Theatre (266 ft × 533 ft).

(3) Those buildings having a square roof structure composed of an orthogonal grid of girders or trusses poised on perimeter supports. The Fifty by Fifty House (50 ft square); the Ron Bacardi Office Building, Cuba (177 ft square); the New National Gallery, Berlin (214 ft square); and the Chicago Convention Hall (720 ft square) are four examples in this category.

FARNSWORTH HOUSE: 1945–50

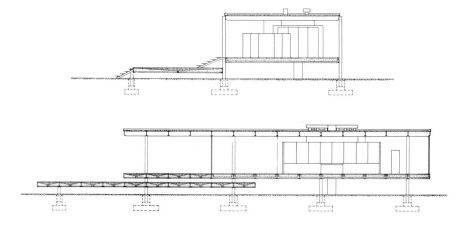

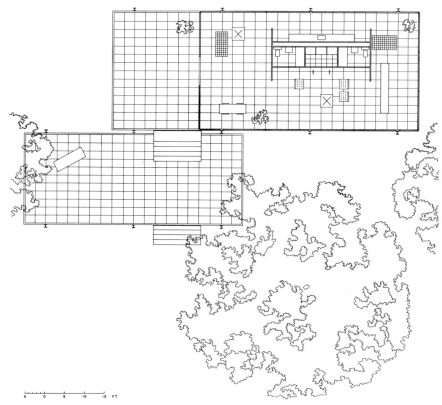

Located in the north-western Illinois prairies near the Fox River—a river that overflows its banks each spring—this country retreat was the first of Mies van der Rohe's clear span buildings to be constructed. Between the two horizontal planes which form the house's floor and roof, the space is subdivided into interconnecting exterior and interior living areas. The interior living area is enclosed by glass and is subtly divided into living, sleeping and kitchen spaces by a free-standing service core. The exterior living area is screened against insects, and is approached by a low flight of steps, broken at mid-point by a floating terrace.

This tranquil pavilion of steel and glass, from which every seasonal change may be observed, is poised above the ground and kept visually open to the landscape. In its relationship to the natural surroundings, there exists no suggestion of a contrived formal composition; indeed, the building's occurrence in the landscape would seem almost fortuitous were it not for the harmony which has been established between the architecture and the terrain. Independent, yet at the same time interdependent, this alliance between the organic and the inorganic creates a convincing image for a technological era.

Overall dimensions of plan	28 ft 8 in × 77 ft 3 in
Gross area of building	2215 sq ft
Column centres	22 ft
Roof cantilever	5 ft 7½ in
Depth of floor and roof channel fascias	1 ft 3 in
Clear height of interior	9 ft 6 in
Height of floor above ground	5 ft 3 in
Height of building	16 ft 6 in

Structure and materials. The building's steel framed floor and roof planes are held 9 ft 6 in apart by wide flange columns so that they cantilever in their longitudinal direction. The welded connections between the columns and the channel fascias at floor and roof are distinguished by the manner in which the two components retain their individual identities, while at the same time the characteristics of the material and its assembly are clearly stated. The skin is composed of steel frames and glazing members and clear plate glass. All exposed steel is painted white. Mies van der Rohe selected the building's materials on the basis of their neutral qualities in order that they would not conflict with the seasonal changes taking place outside the house: the floor, terrace and step surfaces are paved with travertine, the interior core is panelled in primavera, and natural colour shantung drapery provides sun control. These materials, together with the white painted steel, stay within a purposely limited tonal range.

202. Farnsworth House. View from across the Fox River.

203. Farnsworth House. Detail of exterior glass wall.

204. Farnsworth House. Exterior view.

205. Farnsworth House. View of interior from terrace.

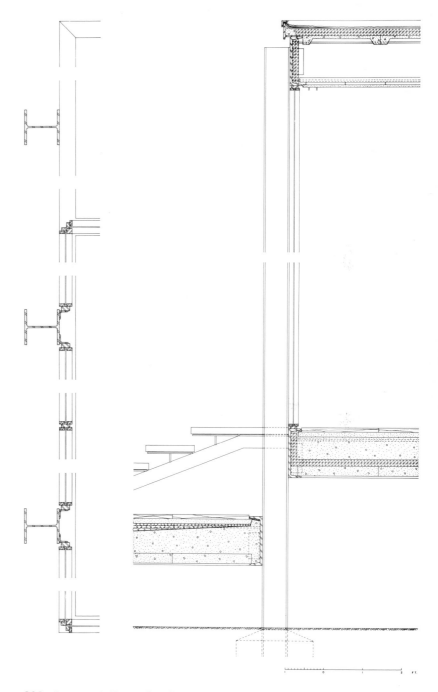

206. Farnsworth House. Details—plan.

207. Farnsworth House. Details—section.

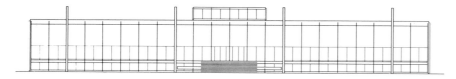

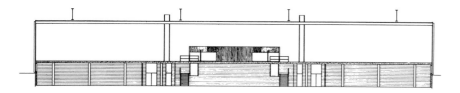

◁ **208.** Crown Hall, Illinois Institute of Technology, Chicago: 1950–6. Exterior view from the south-west.

209. Crown Hall, I.I.T. South elevation.

210. Crown Hall, I.I.T. Section.

211. Crown Hall, Plan of main level.

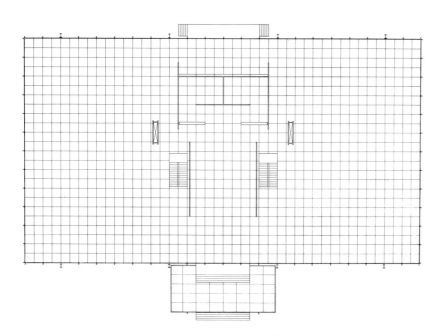

Crown Hall represents the first large-scale realization of Mies van der Rohe's concept for a clear-span/universal-space building. Housing I.I.T.'s School of Architecture and City Planning and the Department of Design, this building consists of a 120 ft wide, 220 ft long, 18 ft high column-free hall, in which the space is subdivided by low free-standing walls and two non-structural service shafts into student work areas, a central exhibition space and an administration corral. The hall is raised 6 ft above the ground in order to provide natural light and ventilation for the workshops and lecture rooms located on the floor below. From the south the building is approached by a broad flight of steps, interrupted at mid point by a floating platform; this structure is separately articulated from both the building and the ground, and upon mounting it one is imperceptibly lifted from the one to the other.

The idea of providing a single large room for the School of Architecture and City Planning's three hundred students was in theory the physical expression of the anti-ivory tower aspects of the curriculum (page 159); in fact this concept proved to be particularly workable; and because a student is not isolated from others who may be further or less advanced in the course than he, he soon becomes aware of his progress in its carefully planned development.

Building module	10 ft
Overall dimensions of plan	120 ft × 220 ft
Gross area per floor	26,000 sq ft
Structural bay	60 ft × 120 ft
Roof cantilever	20 ft
Depth of roof girders	6 ft 3 in
Clear height of main floor	18 ft
Clear height of lower floor	12 ft
Height of main floor above grade	6 ft
Height of building	27 ft 5 in

Structure and materials. Four externally exposed steel bents—located at 60 ft intervals—carry a steel framed roof which in turn cantilevers in the longitudinal direction 20 ft beyond the end supporting members. The building's substructure is of reinforced concrete construction and is independent of the superstructure. The skin is composed of welded steel components and is glazed with clear and trans-lucent glass. All exposed steel is painted black. The exterior stairs are steel framed and paved with travertine. In the interior the floors are of dark grey and white flecked terrazzo, the ceiling of acoustic tile, the walls of the two service shafts are plastered and painted white, and the free-standing walls are panelled in oak.

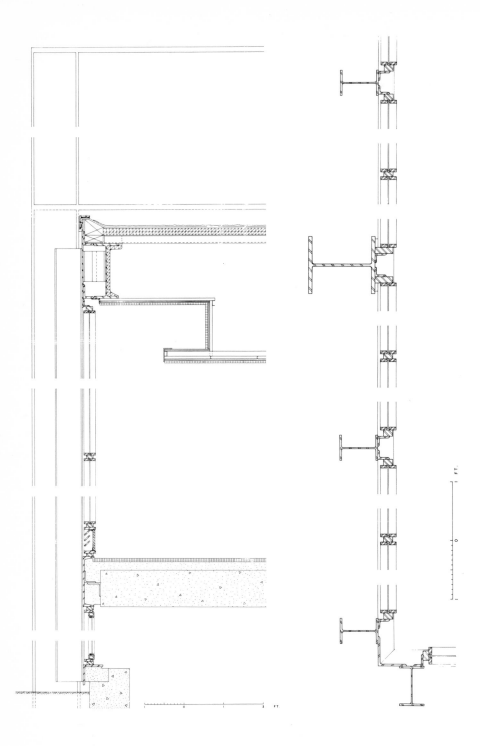

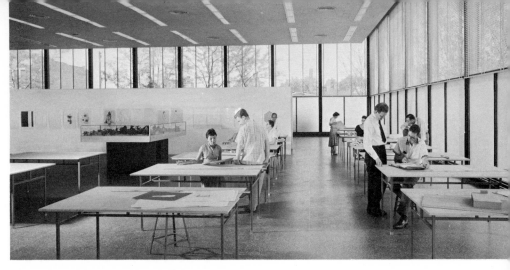

215. Crown Hall, I.I.T. Interior view.

216. Crown Hall, I.I.T. Interior view from central area.

217. Crown Hall, I.I.T. Detail of externally exposed steel bent. ▷

218. Crown Hall, I.I.T. View from south-east. ▷

212. Crown Hall, I.I.T. Exterior view from the south at night.

213. Crown Hall, I.I.T. Details—section.

214. Crown Hall, I.I.T. Details—plan.

219. National Theatre, Mannheim. Project: 1952–3. Exterior view of model.

220. National Theatre, Mannheim. Exterior view of model.

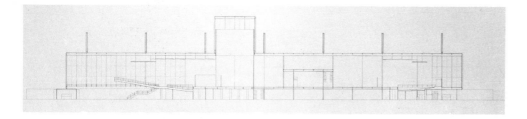

NATIONAL THEATRE, MANNHEIM: 1952–3

221. National Theatre, Mannheim. Section.

222. National Theatre, Mannheim. Main floor plan.

223. National Theatre, Mannheim. Ground floor plan.

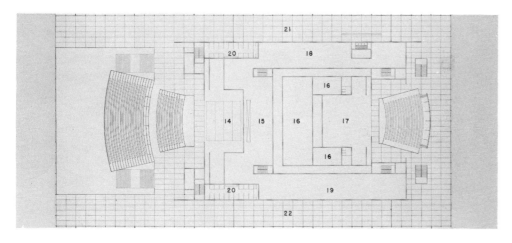

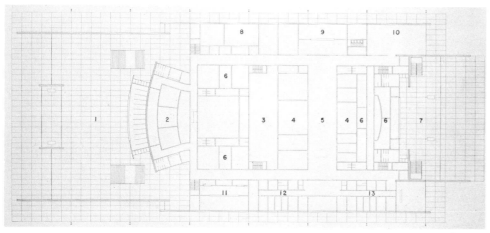

In common with Mies van der Rohe's earlier projects for a Concert Hall (1942) and a Theatre (1947), his proposed Mannheim Theatre building also used—within a column-free space—raised and suppressed seating shells, screen walls and acoustic baffles, to create open stage arrangements which were well ahead of the established theatre practices of the time. The building's elevated and glass enclosed main floor accommodates two theatre spaces, the larger with seating for 1,300 people, the smaller for 500; these two spaces are separated from each other by a free-standing core which houses facilities shared by both. Entrances to the building are located on the floor below—at ground level, where foyers, cloakrooms and the various administration functions are planned. Because the exterior walls of this lower floor are set back from those of the main level, the column-free space above has become clearly expressed.

Building module.	4 m (13 ft 1 in)
Overall dimensions of plan	80 m × 160 m (262 ft × 524 ft)
Gross area of main floor	12,800 sq m (137,288 sq ft)
Structural bay.	24 m × 80 m (78 ft 9 in × 262 ft)
Roof cantilever	8 m (26 ft 3 in)
Depth of steel roof trusses	8 m (26 ft 3 in)
Clear height of main floor.	12 m (39 ft 4 in)
Clear height of ground floor.	4 m (13 ft 1 in)
Clear height of foyer	17 m (55 ft 9 in)
Height of building above grade	18 m (59 ft)

Structure and materials. Seven un-fireproofed and externally exposed steel trusses and supporting columns—located at 24 m centres, carry a steel roof structure which cantilevers in the longitudinal direction 8 m beyond the end supporting members. The building's main floor construction and its supports are structurally independent of this superstructure. The skin is composed of welded steel components and is glazed with grey-tinted glass.

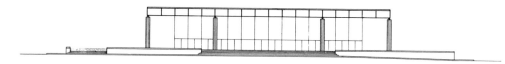

NEW NATIONAL GALLERY, BERLIN: 1962–8

224. New National Gallery, Berlin: 1962–8. Detail view of building.

225. New National Gallery, Berlin. Elevation.

226. New National Gallery, Berlin. Plan of main level.

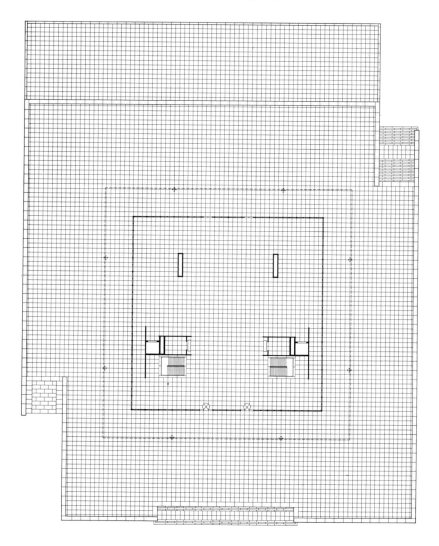

It was inevitable that Mies van der Rohe's personal interest in painting and sculpture should lead him to a sympathetic and fresh approach to the problem of their public display. James Johnson Sweeney recalled that Mies van der Rohe would often visit the Nierendorf Gallery in New York: '. . . he and his friend Karl Nierendorf used to take advantage of the weekend to clear the gallery walls of what was on view and amuse themselves in arranging a special exhibition of whatever they liked particularly, or wanted to see together from Nierendorf's stock. It might be a large selection of Nierendorf's best Paul Klees, of his *Die Brücke* pictures, or a single painting on a large, and otherwise empty wall, a mode of presentation which particularly appealed to Mies.'

In 1942, in his project for a Museum for a Small City (page 97), Mies van der Rohe proposed a solution that was the antithesis of authorized museum practice. In place of a predetermined and relentless progression through a series of containers where art is packaged according to its art-historical slot, he provided a serene and freely flowing neutral space—visually and physically open to the exterior—where paintings and sculptures would not only be seen to their great advantage, but would also assume a new dimension as factors establishing an environment.

At the Houston Museum of Fine Arts, Mies van der Rohe was able to realize these ideas in a practical form. In 1954 he applied the clear span principle to the museum's new Cullinan Hall (page 97) because he believed that this concept would generate rich and varied possibilities not normal in the usual museum. Since Cullinan Hall forms an extension to a typically cellular museum building, this point is made very clearly here.

In 1960 Mies van der Rohe prepared a design for a museum in the German town of Schweinfurt. Although the project was subsequently abandoned, many of its architectural and structural ideas re-emerged in 1962 when he began to work on the New National Gallery for Berlin where the programme requirements were somewhat similar. The New National Gallery is located to the south of the Tiergarten, within the boundary of a new cultural centre presently under construction at Kemperplatz. This complex already includes the 1845 Matthiaskirche and Scharoun's Philharmonie, and five small museums and a state library will eventually complete the project.

The site's east–west slope influenced the decision to plan the building on two levels. On the upper level is a large column-free hall for temporary exhibitions, surrounded by a terrace for the display of sculpture. On the lower level are galleries housing the museum's permanent collections, and spaces accommodating miscellaneous supporting functions.

While the New National Gallery may be seen to represent the culmination of Mies van der Rohe's thoughts on structure and space as applied to the flexible needs of an exhibition hall, at the same time the building presents a puzzling anomaly. There are two distinct concepts of exhibition space employed. Downstairs: a series of fixed spaces, where the permanent collection is shown. While upstairs: one great open room allows painting and sculpture to be displayed in an unlimited number of flexible and stimulating ways.

Building module.	1.20 m (3 ft 11 in)
Roof module	3.60 m (11 ft 10 in)
Overall dimensions of roof	64.80 m (214 ft) square
Area of roof.	4,120 sq m (45,800 sq ft)
Perimeter column centres	28.80 m (95 ft)
Corner cantilever	18 m (60 ft)
Depth of roof structure	1.80 m (5 ft 11 in)
Clear height under roof	8.40 m (27 ft 9 in)
Height of building above terrace	10.40 m (34 ft 4 in)
Overall dimensions of main hall.	50.40 m (166 ft 4 in) square
Area of main hall	2,540 sq m (27,500 sq ft)
Clear height of lower level	4.00 m (13 ft 2 in)
Gross area of lower level	8,400 sq m (90,400 sq ft)
Area of garden sculpture court	1,900 sq m (44,330 sq ft)

Structure and materials. The roof plate covering the large exhibition hall is 64.80 metres square. This welded steel structure is composed of an orthogonal grid of un-fireproofed and exposed 1.80 metres deep plate girders, placed at 3.60 metres centres. The grid is closed on top by a continuous compression plate which is reinforced on its underside with steel ribs to prevent buckling. This structure is poised 8.40 metres above the terrace on eight peripherally located tapered cruciform columns of steel to which the loads are transferred through pin joint connections. Camber was induced at the centre, as well as the four corners of the roof structure to counteract normal deflection, and a slight increase in the calculated structural camber was made in both the centres of the spans and at the corners in order to insure the roof's flat appearance.

To minimize the amount of field work, as much welding as possible was done in the shop. Very large segments of the roof structure were then brought to the site and welded together on the ground. When the whole roof was finally assembled in this manner it was lifted up by 16 hydraulic jacks—two jacks next to each column point. After being raised—with the columns attached and guided into position on tracks as shown on the photograph—slightly above its final height, the roof was lowered to its correct position and the column bases were connected to their foundations. This lifting procedure took about nine hours.

The enclosing skin of the exhibition hall consists of steel members and clear plate glass (a movement joint is provided where the skin's components meet the roof structure). All steel is painted matte black. In the hall's interior, down-lights and spot lights are located in the black aluminium grilles which hang in the roof grid, the two service stacks are faced with green Tinos marble, the free-standing cores are panelled in English brown oak, and the floor and terrace areas are paved with a light grey granite.

Note on the project's history. The building was originally designed in 1962 for the 20th Century Collection of the City of Berlin. Beginning shortly after World War II with a small staff and limited funds, the city built a collection substantial enough to merit a new, permanent gallery. West Berlin was also badly in need of an exhibition hall ample enough to accommodate major touring exhibits. The two facilities were to be combined in what was to be called the Gallery of the Twentieth Century. In 1965 the 20th Century Collection was merged with that of the Nationalgalerie of the Stiftung Preussischer Kulturbesitz. It was renamed the New National Gallery and designated one of the principal structures to be built in the city's cultural centre at Kemperplatz. Land for the new centre had been purchased several years earlier by the City of Berlin in a war-levelled section of the city where embassies and mansions stood before 1939. The first building in the complex, Scharoun's Philharmonie, had been completed in 1963.

The Prussian Cultural Heritage Foundation, which owns all the buildings in the Kemperplatz centre except the Philharmonie, is a national institution, directed by representatives of and funded by all the West German states. With the State of Prussia dissolved by territorial settlements of World War II, the Foundation became a national body in 1961. The Prussian National Gallery was established in 1861 when a Berlin merchant bequeathed his collection to the Prussian King. By 1933 it had become one of the world's foremost collections of post-1800 art. In 1937 nearly 500 of the gallery's finest works were either sold or destroyed by the Nazis. More of the collection perished in World War II. Many works were taken to the Soviet Union after the war and eventually returned to the museum's original home, now in East Berlin.

227. New National Gallery, Berlin. Interior view of main exhibition hall.

228. New National Gallery, Berlin. View of museum terrace.

229. New National Gallery, Berlin. Interior view of exhibition hall.

230. Museum for a Small City. Project: 1942. Interior view.

231. Museum for a Small City. Plan.

232. Cullinan Hall, The Museum of Fine Arts, Houston: 1954–8. Interior view.

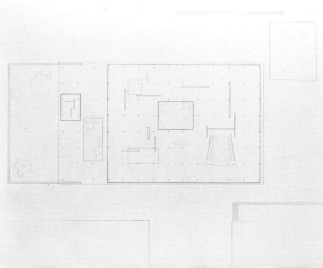

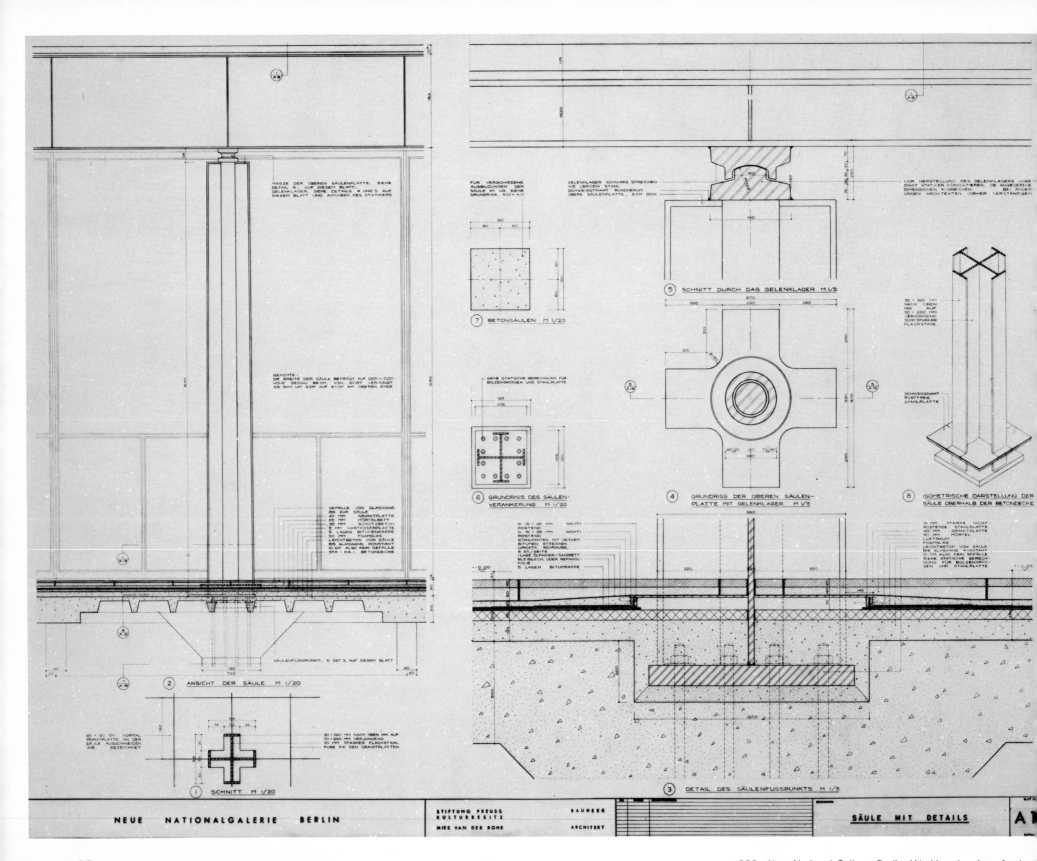

233. New National Gallery, Berlin. Working drawing of colum

234. New National Gallery, Berlin. Exterior view.

235. New National Gallery, Berlin. The raising of the roof and columns into position.

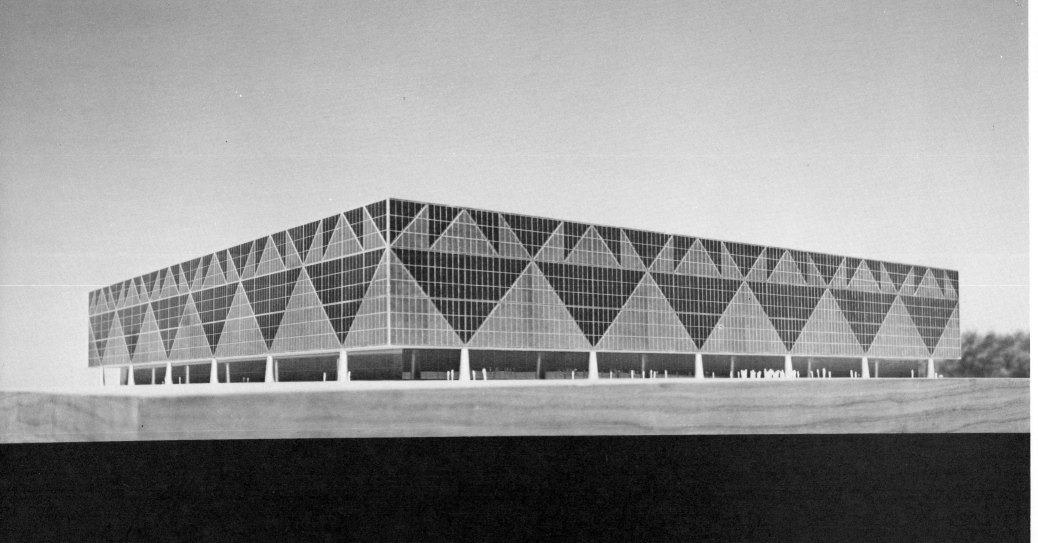

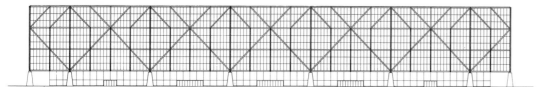

CONVENTION HALL: 1953–4

◁ **236.** Convention Hall, Chicago. Project: 1953–4. Exterior view of model.

237. Convention Hall, Chicago. Elevation.

238. Convention Hall, Chicago. Plan.

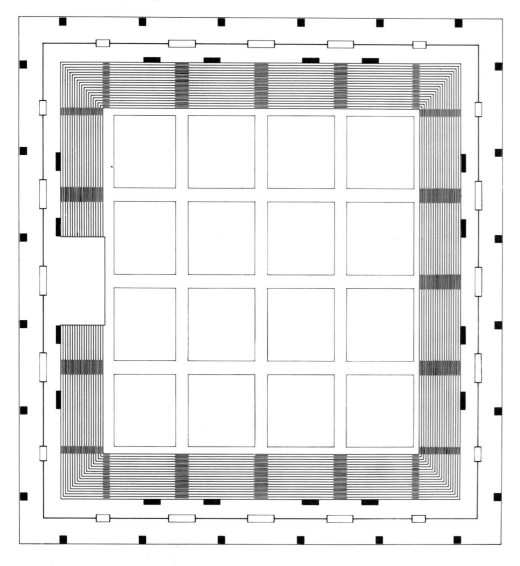

There are over 22,000 conventions held each year in the United States, and more than 1,000 of these take place in Chicago—a city whose geographic location makes it ideal for such events. Mies van der Rohe's project for a Convention Hall for Chicago was sponsored by the city's South Side Planning Board at a time when the construction of such a building was imminent. This project represents the largest of his clear span buildings; its column-free interior permits unobstructed views for an assembly of over 50,000 people; or, alternatively provides 500,000 sq ft of unimpeded exhibition space.

The building consists of two distinct elements:
(1) A ground plane—with the major portion lowered to form the main exhibition floor and surrounding seating tiers.
(2) A 720 ft square steel roof and enclosure structure—supported at its perimeter 20 ft above the ground plane in order to allow access to the hall from all sides.

Public and freight access to the building are on separate levels. The public enters at ground level—as described above—and circulates through the wide foyer that surrounds the hall. Service vehicles, freight trucks and trains gain access at a lower level directly adjacent to the main exhibition floor. The fact that this exhibition floor is suppressed permits a full view of the whole interior upon entering the building.

Even in its unbuilt state Mies van der Rohe's Convention Hall is unquestionably one of his most remarkable works. The building is impressive not only because of its size, but also because of the manner by which its magnitude is visually established and made determinable directly through the structural expression.

Convention Hall

Building module	30 ft
Overall dimensions of plan	720 ft square
Area of roof	518,400 sq ft
Perimeter column centres	120 ft
Corner cantilevers	60 ft
Depth of roof structure	30 ft
Clear height from main exhibition floor	98 ft
Height of building above grade	110 ft
Total exhibition area	500,000 sq ft
Population of a seated assembly	50,000

Structure and materials. The Convention Hall project's 720 ft square orthogonal roof structure is composed of 30 ft deep un-fireproofed steel trusses (assembled from the 14 in series of wide flange sections) spaced at 30 ft centres. This structure is carried at its perimeter on 60 ft deep trusses spanning 120 ft between fireproofed column supports and cantilevering 60 ft at the corners. The building's enclosing skin consists of metal panels set in between the structural members in order that there should be the same expression on the inside as on the outside of the building.

Note on the building's structural development. Mies van der Rohe worked on the Convention Hall project both in his office and with a group of I.I.T. graduate students in his masters' class. The following account of the building is drawn largely from the thesis report prepared in 1954 by Yujiro Miwa, Henry Kanazawa and Pao-Chi Chang under Mies van der Rohe's direction.

The initial structural scheme (239–41) proposed a 2-way truss system spanning 700 ft. The trusses were 30 ft deep and spaced at 20 ft intervals in each direction. The entire truss system and supporting exterior columns were made up from the 14 in range of wide-flange steel beams.

To obtain clearer connections and a simpler structure, three possibilities based on a square proportion for the panel between the chords of the truss were investigated. The first of these proposals used a 20 ft × 20 ft proportion, but the decrease in depth from the initial proposal caused considerable increase in the stresses of the truss members and to answer this proved uneconomical. A scheme using 33 ft 4 in × 33 ft 4 in panels (249a) (three panels per 100 ft as against five in the 20 ft × 20 ft scheme) caused the diagonal bracings from the column to intersect below the plane of the two-way truss structure, which was not a structurally clear solution.

Two possibilities using 30 ft × 30 ft panels were then investigated. One received the support of five columns on each side of the structure and this resulted in end cantilevers of 120 ft (249b). The other was supported by six columns on each side and had cantilevers of 60 ft (249c). While both of these schemes resulted in clear structures, the magnitude of the cantilever in the former caused excessive deflection; the latter scheme was therefore considered the more reasonable. From both structural and architectural standpoints, it was clear, and it was simple to fabricate and erect.

The principle of the two-way truss system chosen may be considered from two points of view: vertical load and horizontal forces. From the vertical load aspect, the principle of this structure is similar to a square slab on peripheral point supports Twenty-three 720 ft flat Pratt type trusses spaced 30 ft apart are simply supported and at right angles is a second rank of similar trusses interlocking in such a way that the total functions as a flat slab. The truss system has a parabolic camber of 20 in at its centre to ensure a straight structure under dead and live loads. There are no moments at any of the supporting points. This is an entirely different kind of structure to the rigid frame principle. The supporting elements which here include the 120 ft flat Pratt trusses between the column points and the 60 ft cantilever trusses at the end of each side are all simply supported.

The upper, or compression chord and the lower, or tension chord of this two-directional system occur throughout; 14 in wide flange chord members are placed with their flanges set vertically, i.e. H-wise. The vertical members connect to the upper and lower chords such that their direction is alternated at every panel point to facilitate the two-directionality of the structure (248).

The weight of the chord members would be heaviest at the structure's centre and lightest at its periphery. To accommodate the moment due to the uniform loads a diagram of the changing weight of the structure's members is bi-convix, the changing members growing flatter with the curve and, therefore, theoretically the weight of all the 14 in wide flange members should be slightly changed from the centre to the edge (250). However, to simplify this the truss system was divided into seven different weights of member by adding plates of variable thickness above and below the horizontal web of the chord members. The diagonal members and the vertical members are lighter at the centre of the structure and heavier at the edge. Above this truss structure the roof slab would be made up of intermediate beams, a metal roof deck, cork insulation and built up roofing.

Wind bracing is needed for provision against the lateral force of both direct wind pressure and suction. In this structure there are two types of bracing, one in the horizontal plane, the other in the vertical (251). The horizontal bracing is located at two levels. One is in the plane of the two-way structure's lower chord where cross diagonal members are introduced in all the panels of the second and third row from the exterior. The other horizontal bracing consists of a 30 ft horizontal flat Pratt truss, its outside chord connected to the columns, its inside chord suspended from the roof structure 60 ft above. Both horizontal bracing systems run along four sides of the structure and connect together at the corners. The vertical bracing is located at a 45-degree angle in the plane of the column supports and these members act only in tension and do not carry any of the roof load. The horizontal bracing at the lower plane of the two-way roof system acts as a stiffener for the entire roof structure, the horizontal bracing at the edge of the peripheral enclosing skin supports and stiffens the vertical mullions while the diagonal bracing ensures stiffnesses for both the column contained within this peripheral enclosure and the roof structure in the vertical plane.

Vertical and horizontal mullions divide the exterior into 30 ft squares and these are further subdivided into three horizontal and six vertical panels by smaller steel members. The ground level recessed glass enclosure is set between vertical mullions which are spaced at 30 ft centres and connect to the interior chord of the horizontal wind-bracing truss.

Two solutions were studied for the peripheral column supports. In both cases, however, the 90 ft column member contained within the peripheral truss enclosure (14 W.F. 426 with stiffener) remaining uniform from the top of the two-way truss system to its intersection with the horizontal bracing truss. In the solution using a steel column (245–6) this upper column is extended as a cantilever and reinforced by the addition of two 14 in W.F. 426 members on each side (thereby employing the greater section of the column to resist wind force) and is terminated at the foundation base plate. The column of the second solution (243–4) was terminated, in line with the horizontal bracing truss, at the top of a concrete pier, 20 ft above the ground. Since the fire code required the base 20 ft of the column to be fireproofed, the latter of these solutions was decided upon.

The peripheral enclosing wall is placed between the structural elements in order that there should be the same expression inside and outside. Glass, marble and metal were studied for this infill. Metal was chosen for its consistency with the metallic nature of the structure itself.

239. Convention Hall, Chicago. Initial structural solution—exterior view of model.

240. Convention Hall, Chicago. Initial structural solution—section and elevation.

241. Convention Hall, Chicago. Initial structural solution—roof plan.

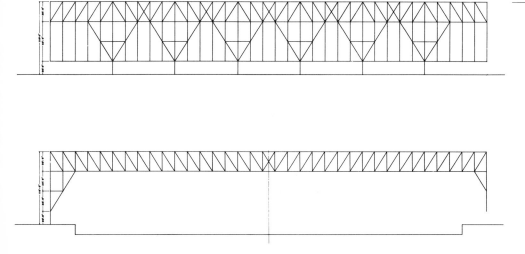

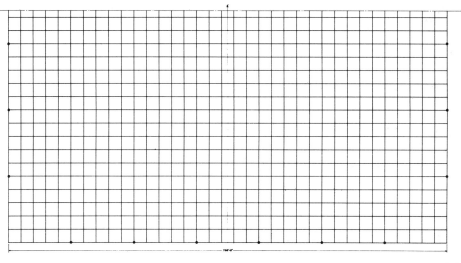

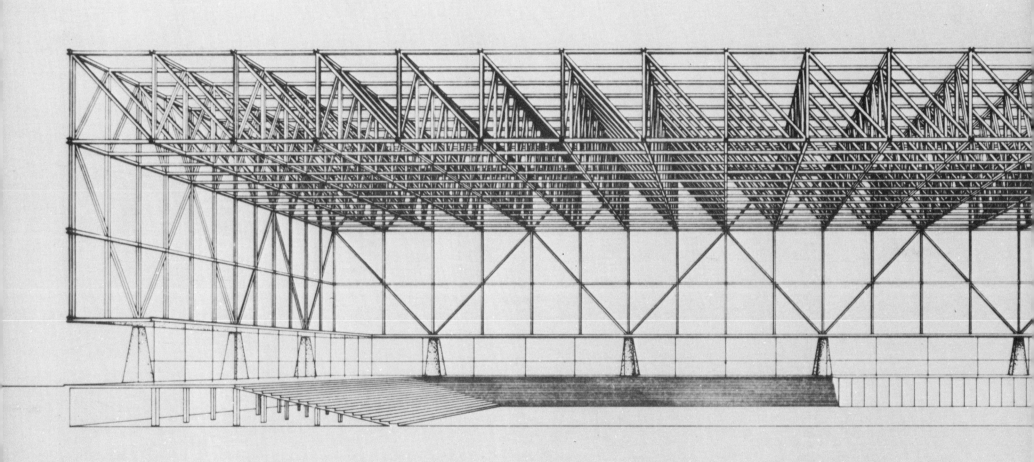

242. Convention Hall, Chicago. Perspective ot interior.

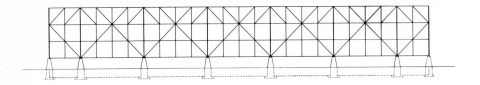

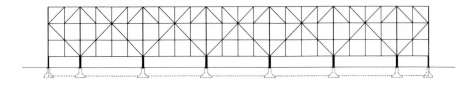

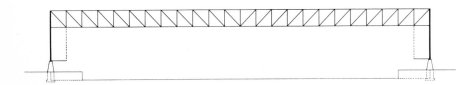

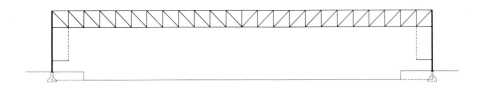

243–244. Convention Hall, Chicago. Concrete pier system.

245–246. Convention Hall, Chicago. Steel pier system.

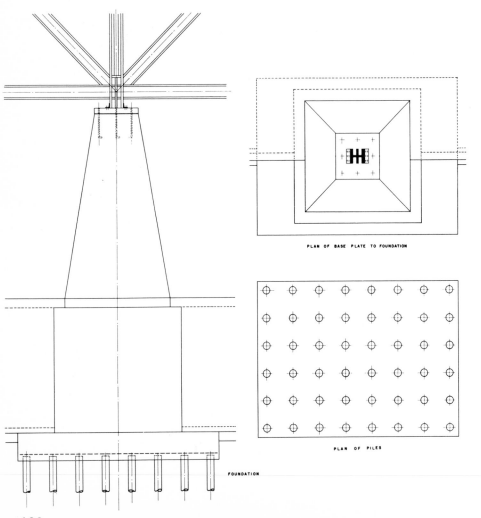

PLAN OF BASE PLATE TO FOUNDATION

PLAN OF PILES

FOUNDATION

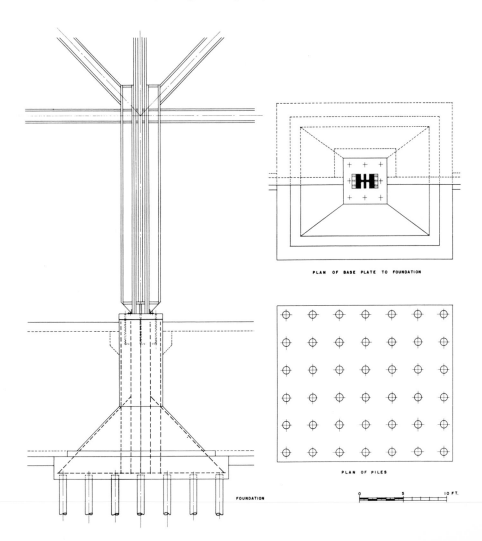

PLAN OF BASE PLATE TO FOUNDATION

PLAN OF PILES

FOUNDATION

0   5   10 FT.

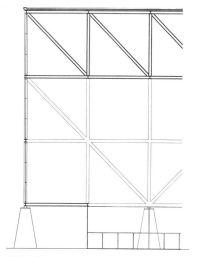

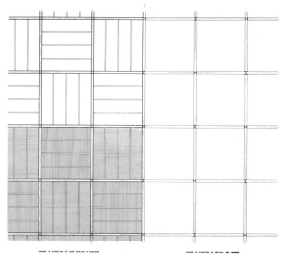

247. Convention Hall, Chicago. Section at edge of building.

248. Convention Hall, Chicago. Roof structure—showing change in direction of purlins and decking (*left*) and of vertical web members (*right*).

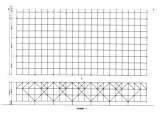
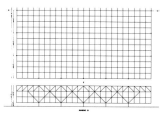

249a, b, c. Convention Hall, Chicago. Three structural proposals.

250. Convention Hall. Plan and section of roof showing changing weight of structural members.

251. Convention Hall. Structural system—lower cord system with horizontal wind bracing (*left*), horizontal wind bracing to wall.

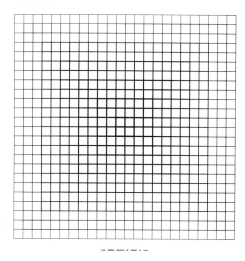

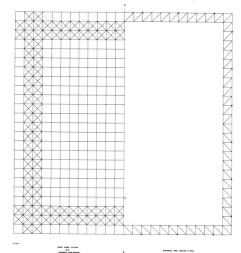

252. Convention Hall. Exterior of model using marble infill panels for enclosing wall.

253. Convention Hall. Exterior view of model using metal infill panels for enclosing wall.

254. Convention Hall, Chicago. Study model of exterior wall using marble infill panels and concrete piers.

255. Convention Hall, Chicago. Aerial view.

Structure, Materials and Detailing

Mies van der Rohe always insisted upon clear structural solutions for his buildings. While he was of the opinion that the majority of structural engineers '. . . know nothing about structure but everything about construction,' he recognized his good fortune in having associated with the American engineer, Frank Kornacher, on such archetypal buildings as 860 Lake Shore Drive Apartments, Commonwealth Promenade Apartments, and Crown Hall. Indeed, in the hands of engineers less receptive to Mies van der Rohe's pristine concept of structure, these early and adventurous works could not have been realized in the form we know them.

This concern for clarity in structural design is apparent in all of Mies van der Rohe's buildings. It is particularly so, of course, in those where the steel structure remained un-fireproofed and fully exposed; a condition which called for the refinement of the standard mill product through the removal of mill scale and other surface imperfections and by sandblasting. Furthermore, the steel manufacturers and erectors were required to approach their tasks with the material's new architectural role in mind: tolerances, for example, were kept to a practical minimum and all welds were ground flush with the steel face. This revelation of steel through a translation of the industry's mill products into finely finished architectural components was one of Mies van der Rohe's most influential contributions to modern building practice.

An understanding of the nature of materials was a characteristic of Mies van der Rohe's way of work. Whether these materials were natural, or man-made, they were always appropriately selected and carefully detailed. In public areas, such as plaza spaces and entrance lobbies, he insisted upon using only those materials which would hold up well under conditions of hard abuse. He used fine marbles, granites and woods whenever the budget would allow; when it did not, his use of brick and other man-made materials would show an identical care in detailing. Often the only difference that may be detected between an apartment or office building which had a high budget from one which had a medium or low budget, is to be found in the degree of fineness of the materials used. The plans were always optimum solutions for their respective function; they were never compromised on behalf of expensive materials.

The point at which one material meets another is solved in Mies van der Rohe's buildings by the introduction of a reveal. The reveal is a small space—an open joint—which permits different materials to meet on the same plane and yet retain a discrete articulation from one another. It allows for the practical necessity of a neutral space where movement due to the varying physical characteristics of different materials and inaccuracies in their manufacture, preparation or setting may be conveniently accommodated. Traditionally, this problem had been solved by the use of a cover strip or moulding.

In Mies van der Rohe's buildings the reveal is an element of the architectural vocabulary. It occurs between floor and wall, between wall and ceiling, and also between panels of wood; and at any point where a construction or expansion joint is located. It also occurs whenever two different materials or parts meet: between door frames and the adjacent wall surfaces; between wall surfaces and recessed items such as illuminated elevator signs, ash trays and convenience outlets.

Because of the magnitude and complexity of many of Mies van der Rohe's later buildings, it became impossible for him to work personally on every item as had been his practice earlier. Nevertheless, he considered it important that every item be carefully considered, and whenever members of his staff showed interest in studying special designs for lighting fixtures, hardware or furniture, he would encourage this. Over the years his office accumulated a wide range of standard designs which were used in many of his buildings and often included in their respective manufacturers' catalogues.

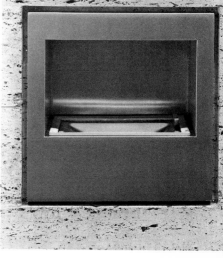

261. Toronto Dominion Bank Tower. Stainless steel illuminated elevator bank sign set in roman travertine wall facing (unfilled and with honed finish). Note reveal.

262. Toronto Dominion Bank Tower. Recessed stainless steel ash tray set in roman travertine.

263. Toronto Dominion Bank Tower. Stainless steel elevator doors and frame set in roman travertine wall facing.

264. Toronto Dominion Bank Pavilion. English brown oak elevator doors, frame and surrounding panelled wall.

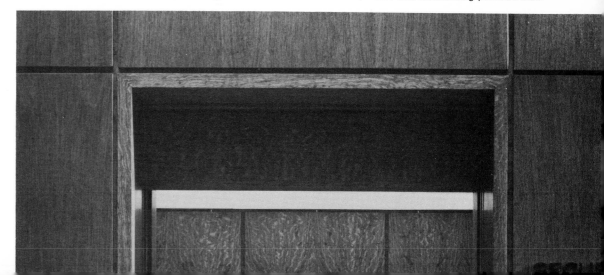

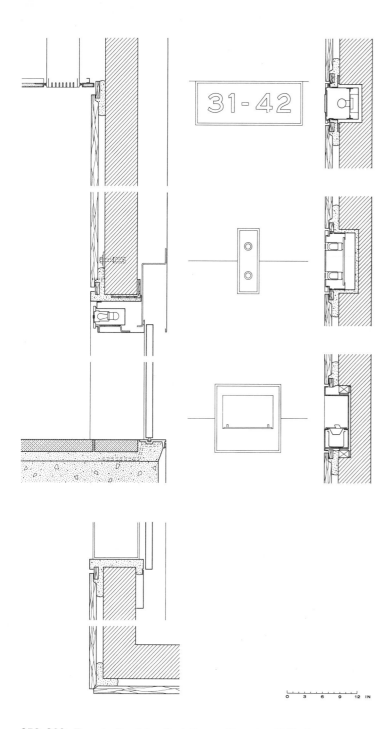

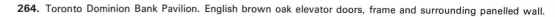

256–260. Toronto Dominion Bank Tower, Toronto: 1963–7.
Ground floor lobby details: **256.** Section through core wall showing elevator door and travertine facing. The floor is paved with granite. **257.** Plan through core wall and elevator doors. **258.** Illuminated elevator bank sign (stainless steel). **259.** Elevator call button plate (stainless steel). **260.** Recessed ash tray (stainless steel).

Three Building Types: Summary

265. Low-rise skeleton framed building: Metallurgical and Chemical Engineering Building, I.I.T. 1945–6. View of interior garden court.

266. High-rise skeleton frame building: 860/880 Lake Shore Drive Apartments, Chicago: 1948–51. Apartment interior.

267. Clear span building: Convention Hall, Chicago. Project 1953–4. Interior. ▷

Mies van der Rohe believed that, from the standpoint of function, a building should satisfy two important considerations: First, it should provide an optimum solution to the client's needs; and second, it should allow individuals the freedom to arrange their working and living spaces as they wish.

He was convinced that a direct relationship existed between a general functional category, its overall space requirements and the structural system which could provide these. For this reason the majority of his buildings fall into one of three distinct types: (1) The high-rise skeleton frame building; (2) The low-rise skeleton frame building; (3) The single-storey clear span building.

Underlying each of these different building types is the dual theme of appropriateness—both to programme and site—and flexibility—both initially and subsequently. In each case only the essential service and transport elements are fixed, and as neutral as possible an overall space is provided in order that the various individual functions and activities may be located to facilitate their optimum convenience and efficiency in operation, and their possible future modification.

Note on building costs. It is not generally appreciated that Mies van der Rohe's buildings were kept within normal budgets and in many cases were constructed at well below those of comparable buildings. The 860/880 Lake Shore Drive Apartments, for example, cost in 1951 $10.38 per square foot—a figure that was 5 to 10 per cent below most conventional apartment house costs in Chicago at this time. Crown Hall at I.I.T. cost $13.71 per square foot in 1955, or 78 cents per cubic foot, a total of $746,850. Apartment buildings such as those which were built in Newark, New Jersey, proved that it is possible today to achieve a high level of design without increasing costs over those of conventional speculative builders' projects. And the large scale urban projects which Mies van der Rohe designed for Montreal (1946–68) and Toronto (1963–9), which cost respectively: $18.66 and $29.13 (Toronto Dominion Bank Tower), were also built within strict budget limitations.

Urban Spaces

From the structural and spatial concepts of Mies van der Rohe's individual buildings, we pass to an examination of the manner by which he brought buildings together, with particular emphasis on the effect his urban spaces have upon people.

From the mid-fifties onwards, there has been a noticeable expansion in metropolitan populations paralleled by a growing affluence in many sections of society. In the cities, these factors have engendered a sudden acceleration in the pace of rebuilding at a time when co-ordinated urban planning is virtually unknown. Circumstances, therefore, have dictated piecemeal development, and the failure of this approach to rejuvenate the urban fabric as a whole is obvious from the parade of unrelated events which characterize most cities today.

In democratic capitalist societies the protection of individual liberties —which, in economic terms, implies competitive free enterprise—and the creation and maintenance of the highest social good, are considered paramount aims. Yet, the desired balance between individual gratification and social well-being is rarely achieved. This failure is particularly apparent in the field of urban rebuilding, where the most flagrant examples of social irresponsibility pass without censure.

To educate public opinion and thereby create a sense of involvement in urban matters should not be by-passed on account of the apparent insuperability of the task. For until such an educated public exists and responsible leadership is established, political opportunism will continue to maintain its control of the planners, and the onus and liability for the urban environment will be left largely in the hands of private owners and developers—men who have usually remained innocent of the prodigious responsibilities involved.

The most effective method of educating public opinion is through good examples of urban planning and building. When such exceptions to the prevailing pattern occur, the degree to which these contribute to the urban environment is directly proportional to the social conscience displayed by the developer, as well as to his architect's ability to comprehend the wider implications of the project upon which they are jointly working.

The schemes by Mies van der Rohe which will now be discussed cover a wide variety of metropolitan site conditions, and while subject to the limitations of today's piecemeal urban development, show, most forcefully, what independent projects can accomplish towards stabilizing the present transitory and anarchical urban matrix.

268. Weissenhofsiedlung, Stuttgart. First scheme: 1925.

◁ 269. Illinois Institute of Technology, Chicago: 1939–59. Exterior view showing relationship between two- and three-storey buildings.

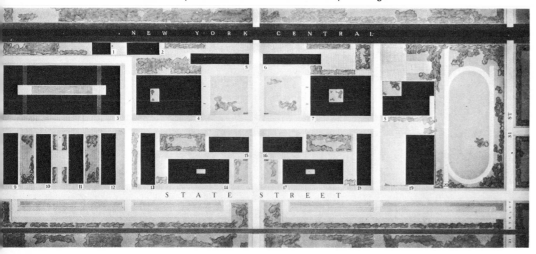

270. Illinois Institute of Technology, Chicago. Master plan.

271. Illinois Institute of Technology, Chicago. Exterior view of a building group.

ILLINOIS INSTITUTE OF TECHNOLOGY—A CAMPUS IN THE CITY: 1939–58

Changing urban patterns frequently place a neighbourhood's more static elements in unforeseen circumstances. Colleges—years after foundation—may find their precincts in the midst of urban blight. Given these conditions, there are two options available to such institutions when the time comes to enlarge their facilities: either they relocate to a more desirable milieu, or they extend their present site with a view to the general rejuvenation of the whole community. This latter course was adopted in 1940 following the merger of Armour Institute of Technology and Lewis Institute into Chicago's new Illinois Institute of Technology.

Mies van der Rohe had been appointed director of Illinois Institute of Technology's Department of Architecture in 1938, and when the Institute decided to build a new 110 acre city campus, he was commissioned to prepare the master plan and to design the buildings. Funds were expected to be available on a somewhat unpredictable basis, with the result that it was decided to house the Institute's various departments in individual buildings rather than accommodate them together in a single structure. Since this would be a residential campus with a population of over 10,000 people, such a concept could be developed into a pleasant landscaped environment for the students, the faculty and their families.

Faced with the problem of maintaining a unity of expression for a large group of buildings accommodating diversified functions whose realization would be spread over a period of ten years or more, Mies van der Rohe chose to use a skeleton frame construction and to express it clearly because, as he pointed out, 'Only a clear expression of the structure could give us an architectural solution which would last.'

Since most of the Institute's departments shared the same general requirements for classrooms, laboratories, drafting rooms, workshops and lecture auditoria, Mies van der Rohe decided to plan the campus on the basis of a three-dimensional structural grid derived from the requirements of a typical classroom—its multiplication providing accommodation for the other functions. The unit chosen was 24 ft square by 12 ft high (the 24 ft structural bay being subdivided into two 12 ft modules for the buildings' steel, brick and glass skin). By covering the whole site with a grid based on this module, columns could be located at the intersections and, because the site was relatively flat, floor heights would be consistent.

In contrast to the typical campus building (page 73), Mies van der Rohe recalled that: 'The Student Union and the Library and Administration buildings confronted us with different problems. I wanted these two buildings to have a more monumental character.

Could that be done with the same means?' The Student Union and the Library and Administration building (page 76) which Mies van der Rohe planned, but unfortunately did not build, were greater in scale than the typical campus buildings; nevertheless, they retained reference to the module and utilized the same black painted steel, buff-coloured brick and clear plate glass vocabulary—a vocabulary which he believed would ensure consistency of character for the campus over the prolonged period of its construction.

The I.I.T. campus covers a rectangular area equal to eight Chicago blocks. In his initial layout, Mies van der Rohe proposed the closing of all but one of the site's heavily trafficked through roads; but as this was not acceptable to the city authorities, a second plan was prepared in which the main arteries remained open.

The campus' principal buildings are grouped symmetrically around a central axis running across the short dimension of the site, but their individual arrangement is asymmetrical. The manner in which these buildings partially overlap each other recalls the treatment of the walls in the Brick Country House and the Barcelona Pavilion, as well as the placement of certain building groups in Mies van der Rohe's initial layout for the Weissenhofsiedlung at Stuttgart. As one walks around those areas of the campus which Mies van der Rohe built,* one notices that the buildings never oppress or impinge— in spite of the fact that the physical distances are not always great. Although these exterior spaces are individually articulated they are never closed—they open freely into adjacent areas; by this means a sense of the larger whole is achieved without loss of local intimacy.

Mies van der Rohe's plan for I.I.T. is particularly interesting for this integration of separate and individually identifiable spaces into a unified totality. Spatial qualities such as these have resulted from the open placement of the buildings; from the clear expression of a generously proportioned skeletal construction—which establishes the module and gives both order and unity to the buildings and the spaces between them; and from the natural counterpoint provided by Alfred Caldwell's landscaping.

* When Mies van der Rohe retired from teaching at I.I.T. in order to concentrate upon his architectural practice, other architects were commissioned to undertake the larger and yet-to-be-completed portion of his campus plan.

272. Illinois Institute of Technology, Chicago. Typical building corner.

273. Illinois Institute of Technology, Chicago. Alumni Memorial Hall: 1945–6.

274. Illinois Institute of Technology, Chicago. Typical landscaped exterior space.

275. Illinois Institute of Technology, Chicago. Metals Research Building: 1942–3.

276. Illinois Institute of Technology, Chicago. Boiler Plant: 1945–50.

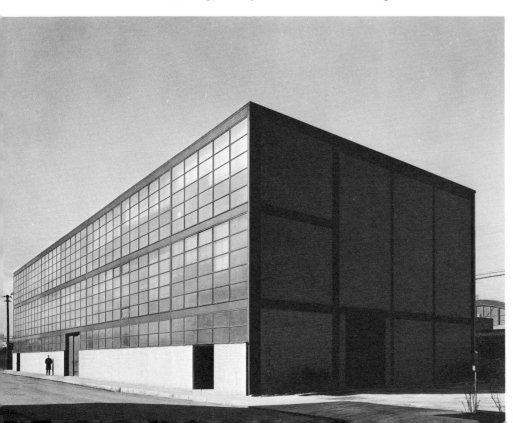

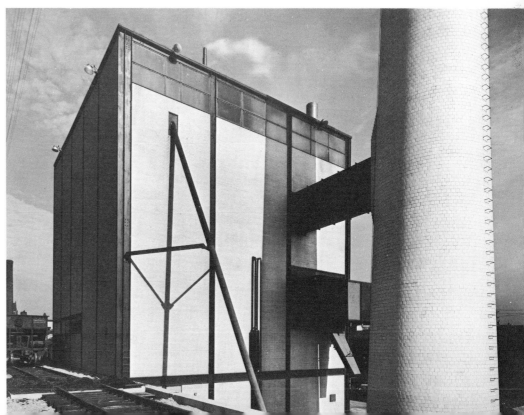

860 LAKE SHORE DRIVE APARTMENTS: 1948–51

◁ **277.** 860–880 Lake Shore Drive Apartments, Chicago: 1948–51. Aerial view from the east (lake side).

278. 860–880 Lake Shore Drive Apartments, Chicago. View from Lake Michigan.

279. 860–880 Lake Shore Drive Apartments, Chicago. Plan at ground level.

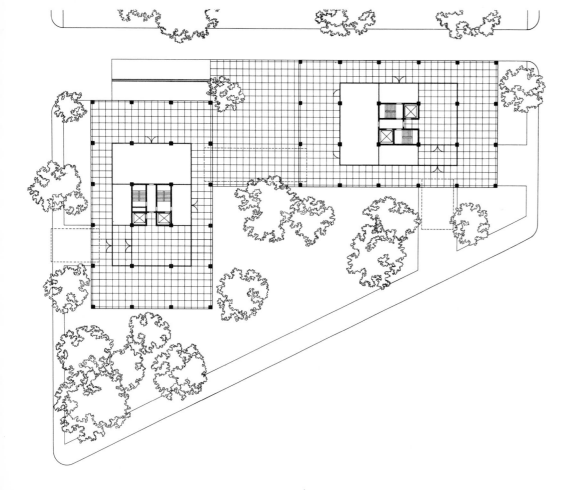

At the 860 and 880 Lake Shore Drive Apartments in Chicago, the spatial concepts which Mies van der Rohe had developed at Illinois Institute of Technology were applied to the field of high-rise structures. Although the 860 site is small, the open placement of the two apartment towers takes full advantage of the site's magnificent location and establishes a sense of almost unlimited spatial extension throughout the area. This, in turn, sets the project's particular character and also permits areas further inland to enjoy contact with Lake Michigan—a condition that is the antithesis of the impenetrable wall of building which lines Chicago's lakeshore in this area.

Of the factors which have contributed towards 860's spatial character, perhaps the following are the most recognizable: The creation of open as opposed to closed spaces due to the non-formal overlapping placement of the towers; the sense of physical and visual penetrability at ground level due to the glass enclosures being set well back from the perimeter columns of the buildings; the easy and inviting access which results from this penetrability and its emphasis by both the contiguity of the ground plane throughout interior and exterior spaces and by the physical link which has been established between the two buildings by the paved terrace and the connecting canopy. On 860's limited site, a new urban pattern was suggested; a pattern that is in scale with the pedestrian, as well as with the fast-moving traffic of a major thoroughfare.

Area of site	0.78 acres
Permissible floor area ratio	see footnote
Proportion of site occupied by building/s	40%
Number of floors below grade	2
Gross area above grade	360,000 sq ft
Gross area below grade	60,000 sq ft
Total number of apartments	288
Underground parking	116 cars
Population/density (people per acre)	768/985

Data relating specifically to the buildings may be found on page 54.

Footnote on permissible floor area ratio. The developer's available financing determined the total square footage to be built; the permissible floor area ratio would have allowed for the construction of considerably more building area.

280. Lafayette Park, Detroit. Master plan: 1955–6. View of site model from eye level.

281. Lafayette Park, Detroit. Aerial view.

282. Lafayette Park, Detroit. Model of master plan. ▷

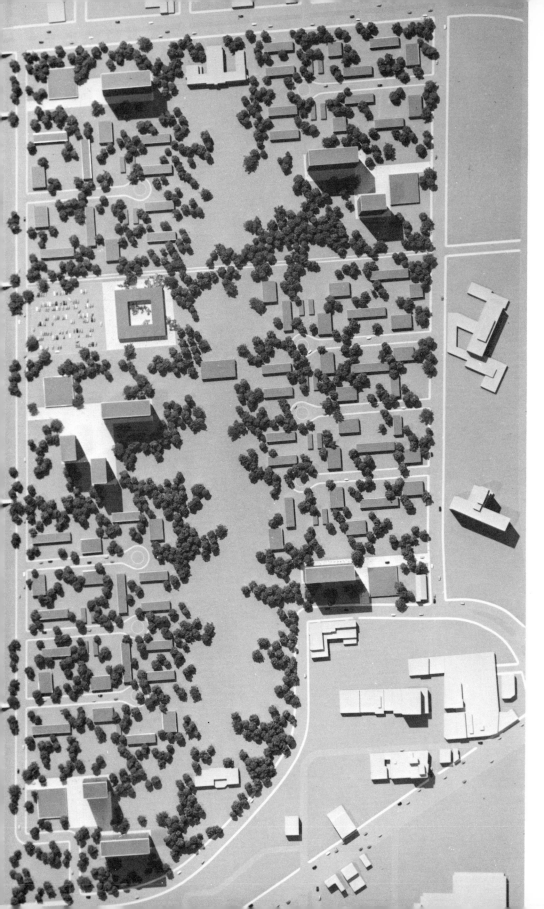

LAFAYETTE PARK: 1955–6

The spatial characteristics of I.I.T.'s low-rise plan and 860's high-rise plan were brought together at the 78 acre urban renewal scheme which Mies van der Rohe and Ludwig Hilberseimer planned for Lafayette Park in downtown Detroit. The exterior spaces, however. now assume a new functional importance as private courts, public gardens, children's play areas, and community park land; and throughout the site Alfred Caldwell's landscaping complements the architecture and furthers the interpenetration of both small and large outdoor spaces.

Access is gained to the various groups of buildings by *cul-de-sacs* from the city roads which surround the site; all traffic is, therefore, local, and none crosses the central park area. The high-rise groups consist of 21-storey apartment buildings planned with underground parking facilities. The low-rise groups consist of one-storey row houses with court gardens, and two-storey town houses. In the low-rise areas a considerable degree of privacy and intimacy has been achieved by the scale of the buildings, the informal and flowing land-scaping, the *cul-de-sac* road system, and the suppressed car parking areas.

The plan of Lafayette Park was the outcome of a unique collaboration between Mies van der Rohe and the city planner Ludwig Hilberseimer. Professor Hilberseimer had always been concerned with the problems of traffic hazards, air pollution, and proximity of living areas to schools and places of work, and these matters became of paramount importance to his city planning theory. In Mies van der Rohe's hands at Lafayette Park, the architectural potential of these ideas is forcefully demonstrated.

By 1956 the first portion of the projected development was complete, but the sudden death of Herbert Greenwald, the project's developer, and the subsequent introduction of work by other architects in addition to that by Mies van der Rohe, was to seriously affect the architectural unity of the project. Nevertheless, the initial concept was strong enough to absorb the alien structures. So that Lafayette Park is today probably one of the most spatially successful and socially significant statements in large-scale urban renewal.

TOWN HOUSES AND COURT HOUSES: 1958. The typical two-storey town or row house at Lafayette Park has a living room, dining room, kitchen, toilet and entrance lobby on the ground floor, with three bedrooms and a bathroom above. A full basement includes space for a recreation room. In addition to this accommodation, the single-storey court houses have a private walled garden court. The structure of these buildings consists of a welded steel frame with steel decking, topped with light-weight concrete. The skin consists of steel components with aluminium glazing frames and clear plate glass. The terminating walls of each terrace are of buff-coloured brick.

The Lafayette Park project was initiated in an interesting way: In 1953 the first portion of a 78 acre plot of condemned property located half a mile from the centre of Detroit was cleared in preparation for the first stage of an extensive urban renewal programme. After a two-year study period, the Citizen's Redevelopment Committee—a body of civic conscious citizens collectively financing urban renewal in Detroit on a non-profit basis who were to act as co-developers on the project— presented a scheme for the site's redevelopment which had been prepared by a group of well-known architects. This proposal failed to attract developers, and it was not until Herbert Greenwald and Samuel Katzin of Chicago took up the options a year later on the basis of a design prepared by Mies van der Rohe and Ludwig Hilberseimer that the future of this important site was determined.

The site was divided into a number of lots, on each of which Greenwald and Katzin took out an option. This arrangement allowed the developer to purchase the individual lots as the construction advanced, while at the same time, giving a commitment to the Detroit urban renewal authorities for the completion of the whole scheme.

283–284–285. Lafayette Park, Detroit. Three views illustrating the relationship between low- and high-rise building groups.

286. Lafayette Park, Detroit. Proposed group of six single-storey court houses.

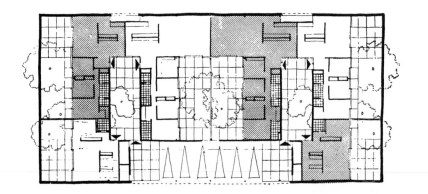

287. Lafayette Park, Detroit.
Two-storey Townhouse: 1958
Ground floor plan.

288. Lafayette Park, Detroit.
Two-storey Townhouse: 1958.
Upper floor plan.

289. Lafayette Park, Detroit. Pavilion Apartments: 1958. Typical apartment floor plan.

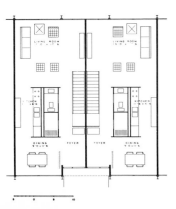

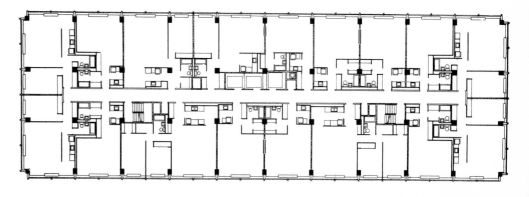

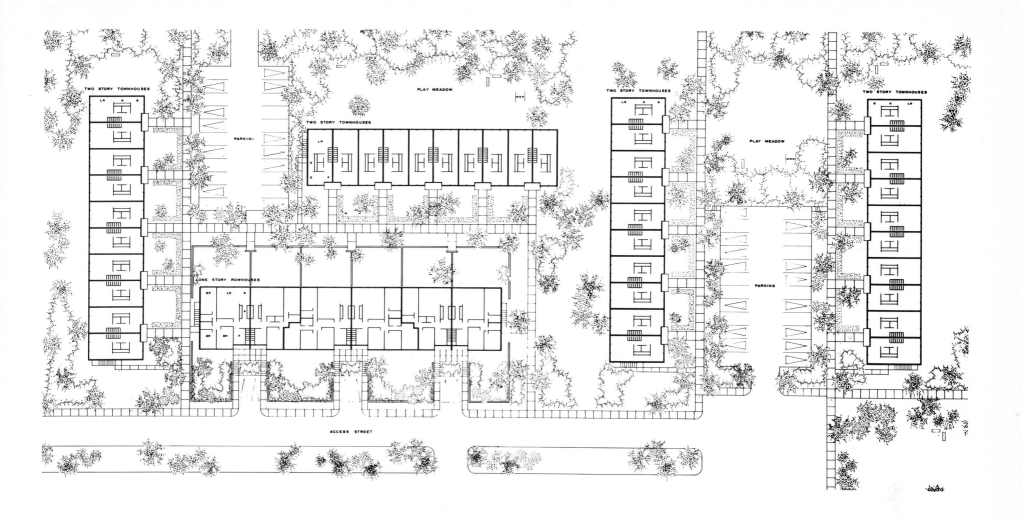

Labels within the plan:

TWO STORY TOWNHOUSES

PLAY MEADOW

PARKING

TWO STORY TOWNHOUSES

TWO STORY TOWNHOUSES

PLAY MEADOW

TWO STORY TOWNHOUSES

ONE STORY ROWHOUSES

PARKING

ACCESS STREET

290. Lafayette Park, Detroit. Low- and high-rise building groups: 21-storey Pavilion Apartments (1958) on the left; two-storey Town-houses and single-storey Rowhouses with garden courts (1958) in the foreground; 21-storey Lafayette Towers (1963) on the right.

291. Lafayette Park, Detroit. Plan of low-rise building group.

292. Typical low-rise housing in Detroit.   ▷

293. Seagram Building, New York. Sketch by Mies van der Rohe of the plaza.

◁ **294.** Seagram Building, New York: 1954–8. View of the plaza from the west side of Park Avenue.

295. Seagram Building, New York. Plan at plaza level.

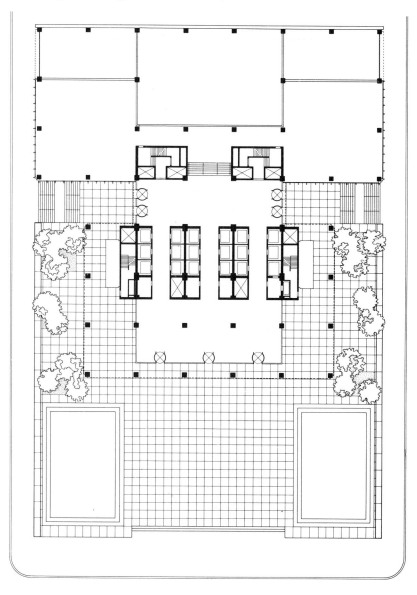

0 10 20 30 40 50 60

SEAGRAM BUILDING: 1954–8

Two factors were to influence the development of the Seagram site: (1) As already discussed on page 61, studies made by the owner had indicated that within the terms of reference of a building of high quality, there would be little to gain economically from filling the permissible space envelope. The actual gross area built was equivalent to a floor area ratio of 10, in contrast to the subsequently constructed buildings on either side of the Seagram site which are in the region of 16. (The present New York zoning for this area permits a basic floor area ratio of 10, with additional increments for set backs on the streets—but not the avenues.) (2) The New York zoning code at that time permitted a tower of unlimited height provided that it did not occupy more than 25% of the site—the Seagram tower became exactly that proportion of its site.

Mies van der Rohe walked along Park Avenue and realized that one could not see any of its buildings from the pavement. After studying the effect of the probable future developments of the neighbouring sites (in the form of typical New York space envelope filling profiles), it became clear to him that the half acre pocket of open space which appeared when the building was set back 100 ft from Park Avenue would contribute in many ways to the project, as well as to the city. Such an open space would establish a point of reference amongst New York's ubiquitous canyons, and, by providing a space for the building to stand in accordance with its magnitude, would give an unmistakable identity to the whole undertaking. Furthermore, at ground level, a public plaza could be enjoyed by anybody who wished to use it, as well as being incidentally beneficial to Seagram's neighbours—in reality it certainly has allowed McKim, Mead and White's Racquet Club across the street to be seen to great advantage.

The planning and structural aspects of the Seagram Building are described on page 61, some aspects relating to the plaza will now be discussed.

To accommodate the slight changes in level which were present on the Park Avenue frontage and towards Lexington Avenue, the granite-paved plaza was raised a few steps above the Park Avenue pavement, and as 52nd and 53rd Streets fall away from Park to Lexington, the plaza becomes further detached from the noise and bustle of heavy vehicle and pedestrian traffic. At these north and south boundaries the plaza is defined by wide marble benches which also act as protective elements at the plaza's edge. The east boundary of the plaza is set by the four-storey section of the building which extends across the full width of the site directly behind the 39-storey tower. The restaurant and bar which are accommodated in this low wing overlook the plaza and in turn provide it with the important element of

visible human activity within the building at plaza level. As is the case with Mies van der Rohe's later urban schemes where he introduced single-storey pavilions on the plazas, there exists at Seagram a readily appreciable interaction between the interior and exterior human activities.

The Seagram plaza is provided with effective foreground elements by two groups of fountains; these help to establish the scale of the space which extends from the street to the building and also give a moment of relief for people walking from street to street. By locating the trees so that they partially screen the buildings on adjacent sites, the plaza environment is contained more effectively. At night, a peripheral band of light illuminates each floor of the building, making both structure and plaza alive for people after office hours. The great popularity of the Seagram plaza is certainly a tangible acknowledgement of the owner's social act and it is interesting to note that this success has had the important side effect of encouraging the development of 'pocket parks' in many areas of New York City.

296. Seagram Building, New York. Detail view of plaza at night.

297. Seagram Building, New York. Detail view of plaza bench and fountains.

Area of site	1.4 acres
Permissible floor area ratio	see main text
Proportion of site occupied by building/s	52%
Gross area above grade	694,000 sq ft
Gross area below grade	157,000 sq ft
Underground parking	130 cars
Population (200 sq ft per person of total gross)	4,255
Density (people per acre)	3,040

Data relating specifically to the building may be found on page 62.

298 and 300. Seagram Building, New York. Two moments during 'Celebration at Seagram Plaza', an inter-media theatrical event presented by Marilyn Wood on 29 and 30 September 1972.

299. Seagram Building, New York. Exterior view showing plaza and open ground floor lobby.

HOME FEDERAL SAVINGS AND LOAN ASSOCIATION OF DES MOINES: 1960–3

This 3-storey structure is located on a relatively small downtown site. The ground floor is devoted to customer services, while on the upper floors, the area not occupied by Home Federal has been allotted to leaseholders. The opening up of a limited area under and around the building as an extension of the pavement (on Grand Avenue the building is set back 45 ft from the property line) has demonstrated that even a small concession to the pedestrian may contribute to the city environment to a degree out of all proportion to its actual physical size.

Area of site.	.65 acres
Permissible floor area ratio.	1.6
Proportion of site occupied by building/s	53%
Gross area above grade	44,500 sq ft
Gross area below grade	14,800 sq ft
Population (200 sq ft per person of total gross)	300
Density (people per acre).	460
Building module	6 ft 8 in
Structural bay	40 ft square
Overall thickness of typical floor	3 ft 7 in
Clear height of typical floor	9 ft 8½ in
Clear height of ground floor	14 ft 7 in
Number of floors above grade	3
Number of floors below grade	1
Height of building	44 ft 7 in
Overall dimensions of plan.	121 ft 9 in square
Gross area per floor	14,823 sq ft

Structure and materials. This building has a fireproofed steel structural frame and is enclosed by a skin consisting of welded steel components, bronze-grey colour aluminium louvres and glazing frames, and grey-tinted glass. All exposed steel is painted black. On the ground floor the soffit is of cement plaster painted white, the cores are faced with travertine, and the floor and plaza areas are paved with Rockville granite.

◁ **301.** Home Federal Savings and Loan Association of Des Moines, Des Moines: 1960–3. View showing effect of the set back from Grand Avenue.

302. Home Federal, Des Moines. Site plan.

303. Chicago Federal Center: 1959–. View showing open treatment at ground level.

304. Chicago Federal Center. (*Left*) 30-storey U.S. Courthouse and Federal Office Building; (*right*) 42-storey Federal Office Building; (*foreground*) U.S. Post Office.

305. Chicago Federal Center. Site plan.

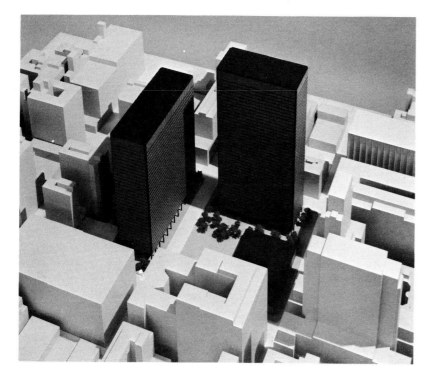

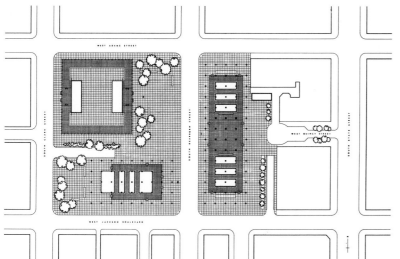

To satisfy their need for extra space and more up-to-date accommodation, the General Services Administration of the United States Federal Government initiated a programme in the 1950's for the construction of a number of new federal administrative and judiciary centres in major cities throughout the country. In 1959, as a part of this programme, Mies van der Rohe together with Schmidt, Garden & Erikson; C. F. Murphy Associates; and A. Epstein & Sons, Inc., formed the Chicago Federal Center Architects in order to undertake the design of new federal government offices and courts in Chicago.

Today, the relationship between government and the people it represents and serves can no longer lend credence to architectural interpretations which harbour representational overtones. By rejecting the representational as well as the enclave concepts, and by treating the Chicago Federal Center as if it were a normal office complex with free access—which is certainly consistent with its functional requirements if they are approached objectively—Mies van der Rohe insured that the development would be properly integrated into the fabric of the city as a whole.

The Chicago Federal Center is located on a block and a half of the city's 'Loop' business district. Past experience had convinced Mies van der Rohe of the need for adequate public space in such congested areas, and he felt this to be of particular importance in a project of this size. He, therefore, planned the center's accommodation within three buildings: a 30-storey office and courts tower, a 42-storey office tower and a single-storey post office (this conformed with the government's time schedule for the project), placing them so as to form two interlinked plazas, the smaller being about the size of the Seagram plaza. Furthermore, by giving the entire ground floor areas of the towers over to lobby space and by setting the glass well back from the perimeter columns (which affords protection from the rain and eases the rush-hour scramble on the pavement), the ground floors have become visually transparent, inducing space to flow freely through the buildings from one street to another.

In the great space formed by the office towers the single-storey post office pavilion (which will be in operation both day and night) establishes scale and assures liveliness at pedestrian level. The first of the Center's buildings to be completed—the U.S. Courthouse and Federal Office Building, is discussed in detail on page 69.

Chicago Federal Center

Area of site.	4.6 acres
Permissible floor area ratio.	see footnote
Proportion of site occupied by building/s	54%
Gross area above grade	2,439,000 sq ft
Gross area below grade	449,000 sq ft
Number of floors below grade	$2\frac{1}{2}$
Population (200 sq ft per person of total gross)	14,440
Density (people per acre).	3,140

U.S. Courthouse and Federal Office Building
Data for this building is listed on page 69.

Federal Office Building

Building module	4 ft 8 in
Structural bay	28 ft square
Overall thickness of typical floor	3 ft
Clear height of typical floor	9 ft
Clear height of ground floor	26 ft
Number of floors above grade	42
Height of building	547 ft
Overall dimensions of plan	116 ft 4 in × 228 ft 4 in
Gross area per floor	26,545 sq ft
Gross area of building above grade	1,115,000 sq ft

Structure and materials. Both towers are similar; a description of the U.S. Courthouse and Federal Office Building may be found on page 69.

Post Office Building

Building module	4 ft 8 in
Structural bay	65 ft 4 in square
Overall dimensions of plan	197 ft square
Mullion centres.	9 ft 4 in
Number of floors above grade	1
Roof depth.	4 ft 2 in
Clear height inside building	27 ft
Height of building	32 ft
Gross area of building	38,800 sq ft

Structure and materials. This building has an un-fireproofed and exposed steel structural frame. The skin consists of welded steel components and clear plate glass. All exposed steel is painted matte black. In the interior the ceiling is of plaster painted white, the floor is paved with Rockville granite, the core walls are panelled with American walnut and the counters are faced with granite.

Footnote on floor area ratio. The Chicago Federal Center is built on government land and is, consequently, exempt from conforming to local zoning ordinances—in this district of Chicago the maximum floor area is determined on the basis of a floor area ratio (F.A.R.) of 16:1, plus additional increments for setting back from building lines etc. The total area of the Center when completed will, however, be well below that which the city ordinances would have permitted.

306. Chicago Federal Center. View of U.S. Courthouse and Federal Office Building from south-west.

307. Chicago Federal Center. Ground floor lobby of U.S. Courthouse and Federal Office Building.

308. Chicago Federal Center. Eye-level view of the three buildings from the north-east.

309. Chicago Federal Center. View of main plaza space.

310. Chicago Federal Center. View of main plaza space from the north-west.

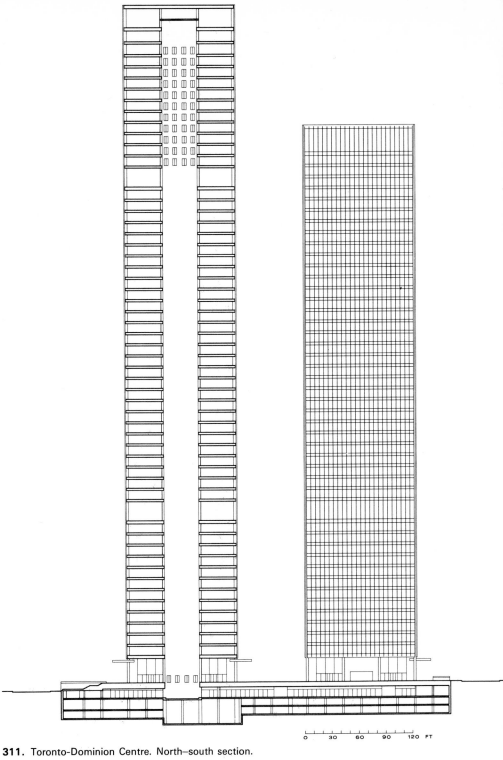

311. Toronto-Dominion Centre. North–south section.

312. Toronto-Dominion Centre, Toronto: 1963–9. 56-storey office building on the left; 46-storey office building on the right; single-storey banking pavilion in the foreground. On the plaza people gather for one of the regular lunch-time concerts.

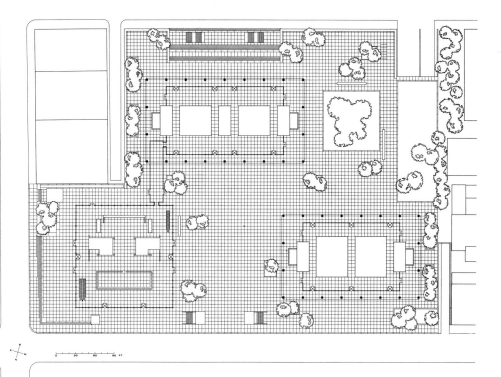

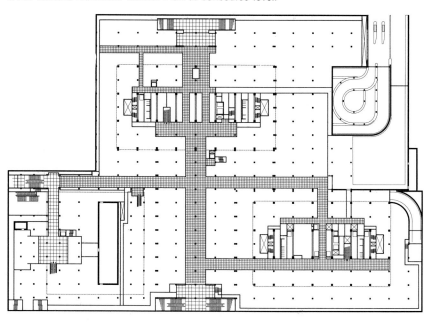

313. Toronto-Dominion Centre. Plan at plaza level.

314. Toronto-Dominion Centre. Plan at concourse level.

TORONTO-DOMINION CENTRE: 1963–9

A decade or so ago, most large-scale commercial developments located in downtown business districts would have been undertaken with little regard for the social wellbeing of the majority of the working population. The introduction of more attractive working environments at the periphery of a city, or further away in the satellite towns, inevitably brought about a re-evaluation of the downtown situation. The result was that some owners and developers began to realize that in planning downtown projects office space must be backed up with such complementary facilities as shops, restaurants, cinemas, theatres and landscaped open spaces—whether the local planning authorities required this or not—if the development was to be a secure investment.

An example of this enlightened planning approach is to be seen in Canada at the Toronto-Dominion Centre. Here, within a 5.5 acre landscaped and traffic-free precinct located in the heart of the city's business and banking district, the Toronto Dominion Bank and Cemp Investments Limited have built over 3 million square feet of multi-tenancy office space (the site coverage maximum), backed up by extensive shopping facilities, a number of restaurants, a 700-seat cinema and underground parking spaces for over 700 cars. This undertaking has contributed to the rejuvenation of the business district as a whole by injecting into it a project where the working and relaxation needs of a daytime population of over twenty thousand people are accommodated within a unified architectural environment.

Design work on the Toronto-Dominion Centre began in November 1963 when Mies van der Rohe (consultant) joined Sidney Bregman (executive architect) and the Canadian firms of John B. Parkin Associates and Bregman and Hamann to form the architectural team for the project. The site is located five blocks north of Lake Ontario and three blocks south of Toronto's new City Hall. Bounded by King, Bay and Wellington Streets—all main traffic arteries—the Centre not only has direct vehicular access from three sides but it is also close to suburban rail and subway services.

The brief called for a total of 3.1 million sq ft gross of office space (to be built in two stages of respectively 1.7 million and 1.4 million sq ft—a division based upon anticipated market demand), and a banking space of 22,500 sq ft, which would become the new headquarters branch of the Toronto Dominion Bank, replacing their existing premises on the site.

Mies van der Rohe was convinced that the banking function would require a freer and more flexible type of space than could be provided by its incorporation in an office building—where both functions would be penalized. He, therefore, decided to accommodate this complex function in a separate single-storey clear span building and to develop the site with this low structure and the two office towers in such a way that a number of individually identifiable yet interlinked public plaza spaces would be created at ground level. An underground shopping concourse was then developed over the whole site, connecting the two towers with the banking pavilion and with the two-level parking facility below. A detailed description of the 56-storey Toronto Dominion Bank Tower appears on page 65.

Area of site	5.5 acreas
Permissible floor area ratio	12:1
Proportion of site occupied by building/s	33%
Number of floors below grade	3
Gross area above grade	2,890,000 sq ft
Gross area below grade	700,000 sq ft
Underground parking	700 cars
Population (200 sq ft per person of total gross)	18,000
Density (people per acre)	3,280

Toronto Dominion Bank Tower
Data for this building is listed on page 65.

Royal Trust Tower

Building module	5 ft
Structural bay	30 ft × 40 ft
Overall thickness of typical floor	3 ft
Clear height of typical floor	9 ft
Clear height of ground floor	26 ft
Number of floors above grade	46
Height of building	600 ft
Overall dimensions of plan	124 ft 3 in × 214 ft 3 in
Gross area per floor	26,530 sq ft
Gross area of building above grade	1,180,800 sq ft

Structure and materials. Both towers are similar; a description of the Toronto Dominion Bank Tower may be found on page 65. On the underground shopping concourse the shop fronts consist of black aluminium fascias and sliding screens and clear plate glass, the ceiling has fields of acoustic tile, and the floor is paved with a dark green flecked terrazzo.

Banking Pavilion (Main Branch, The Toronto Dominion Bank)

Building module	5 ft
Number of floors above grade	1
Number of floors below grade	1
Overall dimensions of plan	150 ft square
Module of clear span roof structure	10 ft
Roof depth	5 ft
Clear height inside pavilion	25 ft 6 in
Height of building	30 ft 8 in
Gross area of pavilion	22,500 sq ft
Module of perimeter supports	10 ft

Structure and materials. The building has a clear span welded steel waffle roof structure—un-fireproofed and exposed—comprising 4 ft 6 in deep 150 ft long girders and 10 ft long diaphragm beams spanning both directions at 10 ft centres. This structure is supported at the periphery on cruciform-shaped steel columns located at each girder line. The skin consists of steel subframes and glazing members set between the columns and glazed with bronze-grey tinted glass. All exposed steel is painted matte black. In the interior the ceiling consists of low-brightness fluorescent lighting fixtures set into the structural roof grid, the floor is paved with St. John's grey granite, the two service shafts and the counters are faced with green Tinos marble, and the cores are panelled with English brown oak.

315. Toronto-Dominion Centre. View at night from King Street. ▷

316. Toronto-Dominion Centre. Interior view of banking pavilion.

317. Toronto-Dominion Centre. View of the banking pavilion from the corner of Bay and King Streets.

318. Toronto-Dominion Centre. Shopping concourse.

319. Toronto-Dominion Centre. Shopping concourse.

320. Toronto-Dominion Centre. Wellington Street steps.

321. Toronto-Dominion Centre. Summer lunch-hour on the plaza. ▷

322. Toronto-Dominion Centre. The cinema entrance lobby.

323. Toronto-Dominion Centre. The cinema auditorium.

WESTMOUNT SQUARE: 1965–8

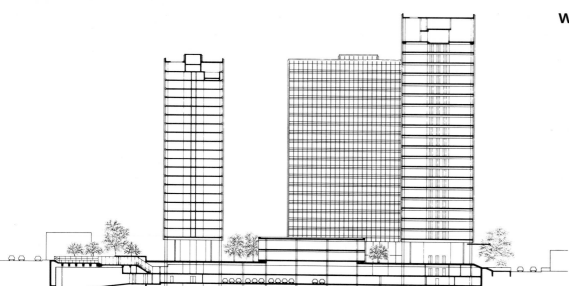

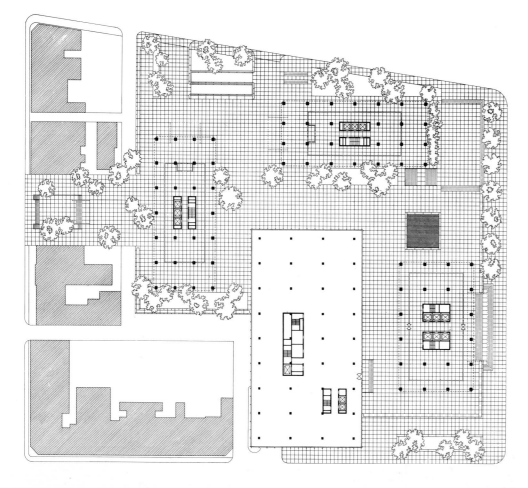

The incorporation of both living and working activities within a single large-scale urban development would appear to be a sound and meaningful planning concept; yet, because of restrictive zoning ordinances, high land values and inequitable tax assessments, this has rarely been attempted. Seen within this context, Westmount Square stands as a somewhat unique example, and particularly so when one considers the fact that its composition was determined largely on the basis of market research—followed by the appropriate by-law amendment from the city authorities. This project's incorporation of such complementary functions as apartments, office space, shops, restaurants, a cinema, car parking and a subway station—all within a 3.5 acre landscaped and traffic free precinct—uncompromisingly demonstrates that a balanced urban environment can be made both desirable and economically feasible.

Westmount Square is located two miles to the west of Montreal's downtown centre. Its present stage comprises two 21-storey apartment towers, one 21-storey office tower and a two-storey office structure. The ground level is developed as a landscaped plaza, with a shopping concourse and parking facility located below. Mies van der Rohe worked on the Westmount Square development in association with the Canadian architects: Greenspoon, Freedlander, Dunne, Plachta and Kryton.

◁ **324.** Westmount Square, Montreal: 1965–8. Distant view of Westmount Square.

325. Westmount Square. Section through project.

326. Westmount Square. Plan at plaza level.

Westmount Square

Area of site.	3.56 acres
Permissible floor area ratio	7:1
Proportion of site occupied by building/s	40%
Gross area above grade	740,500 sq ft
Gross area below grade	465,300 sq ft
Number of floors below grade	3
Total gross office area	238,370 sq ft
Total number of apartments	226
Underground concourse: net shop and restaurant area	125,830
Underground parking	650 cars
Population (offices, apartments and below plaza)	4,600
Density (people per acre)	1,300

Office building

Building module	5 ft 3 in
Structural bay	26 ft 3 in square
Overall thickness of typical floor	3 ft 1 in
Clear height of typical floor	8 ft 6 in
Clear height of ground floor	23 ft
Number of floors above grade	22
Height of building	273 ft
Overall dimensions of plan	83 ft 6 in × 136 ft
Gross area per floor	11,350 sq ft
Gross area of building above grade	238,400

Low-rise office building

Building module	8 ft 9 in
Structural bay	26 ft 3 in × 35 ft
Clear height of typical floor	9 ft 6 in
Number of floors above grade	2
Height of building	26 ft 10 in
Overall dimensions of plan	125 ft × 230 ft
Gross area per floor	28,750 sq ft
Gross area of building above grade	57,500 sq ft

Apartment buildings

Building module	5 ft 3 in
Structural bay	21 ft × 26 ft 3 in
Overall thickness of typical floor	1 ft 1 in
Clear height of typical floor	8 ft 6 in
Clear height of ground floor	23 ft
Number of floors above grade	21
Height of building	228 ft
Overall dimensions of plan	67 ft 6 in × 162 ft
Gross area per floor	10,930 sq ft
Gross area of building above grade	222,325 sq ft (each)
Number of apartments	108 and 118

Structure and materials. The buildings are of reinforced concrete waffle slab construction and are enclosed with skins consisting of black aluminium components and grey-tinted glass. On the ground floors the soffits are of cement plaster painted white, and travertine is used to face the cores and to pave the lobby floors and plaza areas.

327. Westmount Square. (*Left and right foreground*) 21-storey apartment buildings; (*centre*) 2-storey office pavilion, 22-storey office building.

328. Westmount Square. View of model. **329.** Westmount Square. Plaza view of building

330. A New City Square and Office Tower, London: 1967–. The new city square boarded by Mies van der Rohe's 20-storey office tower on the left, Lutyens' Midland Bank (1936) in the centre, and Dance's Mansion House (1739) and the Church of St. Stephen Walbrook by Wren and Vanbrugh (1672) on the right.

A NEW CITY SQUARE AND OFFICE TOWER IN THE CITY OF LONDON: 1967–

331. A New City Square and Office Tower. Aerial view of existing site conditions.

332. A New City Square and Office Tower. Aerial view of model showing proposed development.

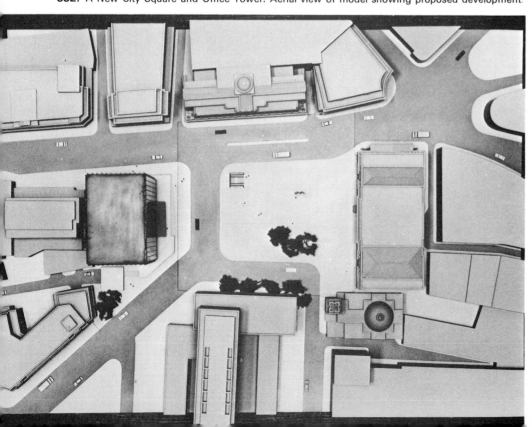

The new foreign branch headquarters of Lloyds Bank and the development of the adjacent area immediately to the west of the Mansion House was the result of a study upon which Mies van der Rohe and Lord Holford collaborated. The overriding consideration in the planning of this project was the presence under Queen Victoria Street of one of London's underground railway tunnels. This tunnel divided the site diagonally and since bridging over it would have been economically prohibitive, the choice of location for the new office building inevitably fell to the western and larger of the two triangular areas which the tunnel created. At this location it was possible to build a 20-storey tower, rectangular in plan, and with a typical floor area of 10,000 sq ft, which could accommodate the requirements of Lloyds Bank. With the remainder of the site now free it became feasible to introduce a landscaped public plaza and an underground shopping concourse with direct access to the Bank underground station, as well as improve the junction between Queen Victoria Street and Poultry.

The office tower was carefully sited so that all of the traditional views of St. Paul's Cathedral are respected. From the distance, the building will take its place as one structure in a group of high buildings which now exist in this area of London. From close up, the building's enclosing skin of bronze and glass will complement the stonework of the adjacent structures, reflecting their architectural features and adding to their traditional materials those of today.

333. A New City Square and Office Tower. Eye-level view of proposed square.

334. A New City Square and Office Tower. Typical floor plan of office tower.

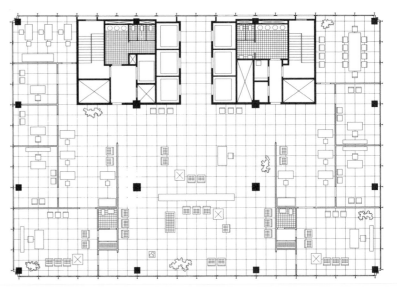

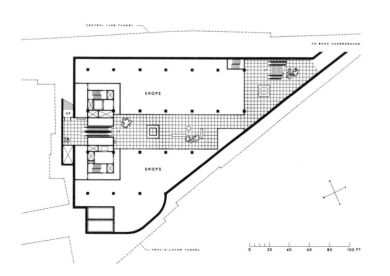

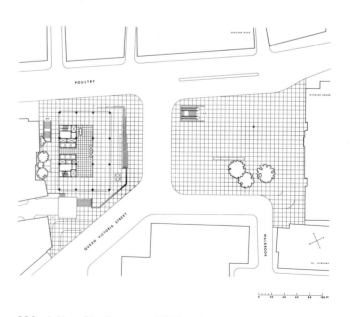

335. A New City Square and Office Tower. Plan at shopping concourse level.

336. A New City Square and Office Tower. Plan at ground level.

A New City Square and Office Tower

Area of site . . . . .8 acres
Permissible floor area ratio 5.5:1
Proportion of site occupied by building/s 26.2%
Gross area above grade . . . . 193,800 sq ft
Gross area below grade . . . . 67,500 sq ft
Underground concourse: net shop and restaurant area . . . . . . 23,000 sq ft
Underground parking . . . . 8 cars
Population (200 sq ft per person of total gross) 1300
Density (people per acre) 1620

Building module . . . . 6 ft 6 in
Structural bay . . . . 26 ft × 39 ft
Overall thickness of typical floor . . . . 3 ft
Clear height of typical floor . . . . 10 ft
Clear height of ground floor . . . . 24 ft 6 in
Number of floors above grade 20
Number of floors below grade 3
Height of building . . . . 290 ft 6 in
Overall dimensions of plan . . . . 82 ft × 121 ft
Gross area per floor . . . . 9,916 sq ft
Ratio of core to gross area* 22%

* Core: total area occupied by passenger and service lift shafts and lobbies, mechanical ducts, telephone and electric rooms, toilets, fire stairs.

Structure and materials. This building has a fireproofed steel structural frame and is enclosed with a skin consisting of bronze components and bronze-grey tinted glass. On the ground floor the soffit is of pinkish-grey glass mosaic, the cores are faced with travertine, and the lobby floor and plaza areas are paved with Cornish granite.

City planning note. The considerations behind the proposal for a public open space equivalent in size to Leicester Square include: The significant location of the site at the geographical centre of the City of London, the number of the city's main pedestrian routes that cross at this point, and the presence of the Church of St. Stephen Walbrook by Wren and Vanbrugh (1672), George Dance's Mansion House (1739), and Sir Edwin Lutyens' Midland Bank (1936). These three buildings, together with the new Lloyd's Bank building, surround the square and will establish its character and provide both a setting and forecourt for the Mansion House.

Note on public exhibition of project. Anticipating a requirement of the British Government's new town planning regulations, a public exhibition comprising models, photomontages and material samples of the New City Square and Office Tower project was held at the Royal Exchange during October 1968. 30,000 people visited the exhibition, and of the 3,325 who accepted the City Corporation's invitation to express an opinion in writing, the majority were in favour of the project. Notwithstanding individual approval or disapproval of the project, one of the most frequently mentioned comments recognized the fact that there had been a public exhibition of the scheme *before* town planning permission had been granted by the local authority, at which people had been invited to comment, and this was greatly appreciated:

Comment No. 69. MERCHANT BANKING (Investments): I am an American, grown accustomed to mass urban redevelopment being forced upon people without warning, and I am extremely impressed by the consideration and quality of this exhibit. I won't comment on the actual design because it is irrelevant and a matter of individual taste. But what is important, I think, is to accustom the people to what they're going to have to live with for the rest of their lives. You have taken consideration for people's natural conservations, and have eased the shock of change. Hence I commend this exhibit highly. And when the project gets built, I'll probably commend that too.

The comments in general tended to fall into one of three categories: those who were against the whole project; those who had reservations about the building but were in favour of the open landscaped square; and those who were enthusiastically for the whole project going ahead as proposed. Of those expressing opinions which were against the project as a whole, by far the most frequently mentioned concern was that it would not be in keeping with the traditional character of the City of London—a pre-war phenomenon that is rapidly disappearing from the scene:

Comment No. 2691. RETIRED: Poor Old London! She is being wantonly pulled down stone by stone in order to throw up the modern monstrosities that are so extremely ugly and characterless and unnecessary. Friends of mine from other countries are as distressed as I am that English people should permit such desacration to take place. I hope, with all my heart, that this plan *will not* be permitted.

By far the largest proportion of comments described the building as 'just another up-ended matchbox', but at the same time these people were enthusiastic about the square and the underground shopping concourse. Many, in fact, had clearly understood that this open public space was made possibly only by stacking the office accommodation in a tall building:

Comment No. 715. SECRETARY: I hate tall square blocks, nevertheless on balance the suggested scheme is highly commendable. The enjoyment of additional light and unopposed views of the Mansion House etc. will outweigh one 'monster on stilts', and we can appreciate the City's architectural beauties far more when they are interspersed with spaciousness instead of Stigeon gloom. After this summer, I feel sure women will appreciate an underground shopping concourse! So far as the view of St. Paul's is concerned, weighing up the delight of picking out well-known landmarks from vantage points such as Hampstead Heath, I feel that working conditions for those coming into the City are deteriorating yearly, and this square would in total benefit the greatest number.'

Those people who were in favour of the project as a whole often referred to the need in the City of London for both a good building and an open public square as examples for future developments:

Comment No. 2478. COMPUTER PROGRAMMER: I am whole-heartedly in favour of this project, both on practical, social and purely aesthetic grounds. In this part of the city, any opening out is welcomed. The argument that such openings destroy the character of the city should not be entertained, as a static character, prevented from altering to suit present needs, is soon a stagnant character. People are used to either living in open spaces, or having easy access to such spaces, and work more efficiently, although they may be unconscious of it, where such spaces are available. A short visit to such a square as this can often revive the most jaded office worker, to the benefit of employee and employer. On wider social grounds, I feel this building and square would be a superb example for British architects and planners of what can be done to save city areas blighted by old and mediocre new buildings. Many British laymen are prejudiced against towers in general, having seen so many poor ones, and this building will be an example to them of what towers should be like. In the aesthetic field individual opinion only is valid, so speaking purely for myself, I must express great admiration for such a perfect monument to the best of modern thought. In future years much of present achievement will be dismissed as mediocre and of appeal only to its period of inception, but this will go on, like the best of Classical and Renaissance building, to show that some at least had thought for posterity.

On 22 May 1969 the Common Council of the City of London conditionally approved the project requiring that the office building and the square be carried out as a continuous staged operation, in accordance with the present proposals and incorporating the present high quality of materials and design.

337. A New City Square and Office Tower. The shopping concourse links the office tower with the Bank underground railway station.

338. A New City Square and Office Tower. The exhibition held at The Royal Exchange during October 1968 was attended by over 30,000 people.

339. A New City Square and Office Tower. The Mansion House in the left foreground. ▷

Urban Spaces: Plaza Detailing

340. Plaza furniture at the Toronto-Dominion Centre.

341. Plaza furniture at the Chicago Federal Center.

342. Solution to sloping streets around the Seagram Building plaza.

Mies van der Rohe consistently worked towards solutions which would provide the most direct way of entering a building at street level. Whenever existing grades permitted, he would make a single horizontal plane from the pavement, across the plaza, into the entrance lobby. He would not employ arbitrary changes in level. When the grade levels varied around a site and required the introduction of steps, these were designed for ease in ascent. When such grade variations called for protective barriers at the edge of the plaza, this problem was often solved by edging the plaza with a bench of marble or granite.

These and other items with which one has close visual and physical contact, such as paving and plaza furniture, received the same care in material selection and detailing as did the buildings. This overall quality control resulted in a total architectural unity for a project, and it established an environment at ground level which, because it was in scale with people, became readily assimilated into the general fabric of the city.

At night, the plaza spaces are illuminated principally by light reflected from the high and open ground-floor areas of the buildings. Trees and fountains are independently illuminated from lighting sources located in the planting pits and reflecting pools. This subtle illumination makes the plaza spaces pleasant, inviting and lively at night.

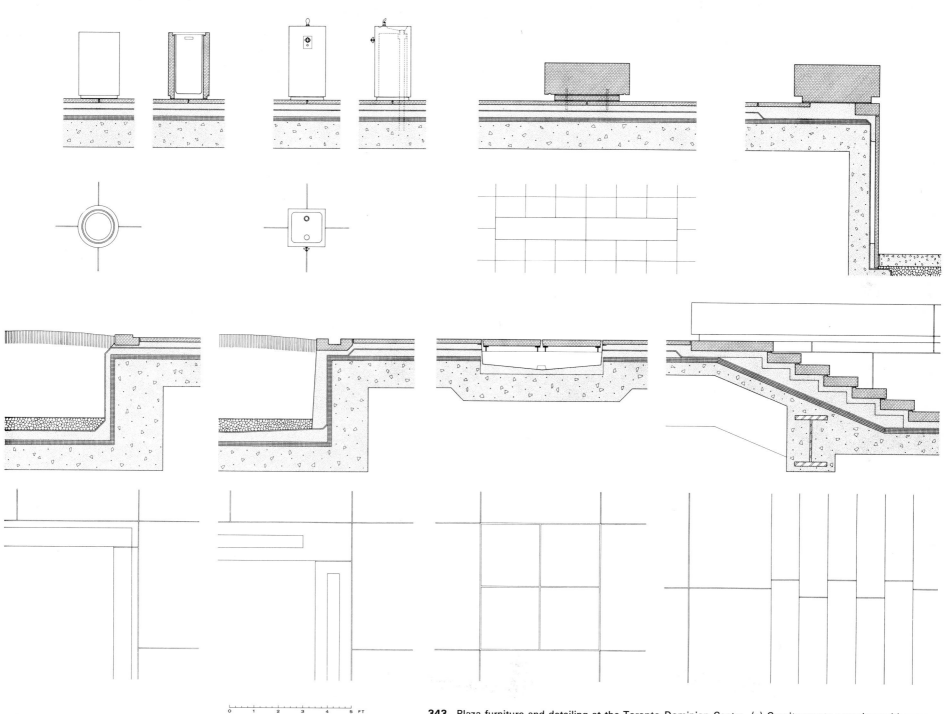

343. Plaza furniture and detailing at the Toronto-Dominion Centre. (a) Granite waste container with removable metal bin. (b) Granite drinking fountain with bronze fittings. (c) Free-standing plaza bench. (d) Bench forms barrier at plaza edge. (e) (f) Details of plaza planting pits. (g) Typical plaza drain. (h) Typical plaza steps.

Waynesburg College Library
Waynesburg, Pa. 15370

Urban Spaces: Landscaping

344. Toronto-Dominion Centre.

345. Lafayette Park, Detroit.

'Landscaping must follow the lines of the free growing tree.' This conviction stated by the American landscape architect Jens Jensen (1860–1951) deeply affected Alfred Caldwell's approach to landscaping. His planting plans for Mies van der Rohe's projects show that he found a parallel between Jensen's insistence on the integrity of nature and Mies van der Rohe's insistence on the honest expression of a building's structure. The regimented and the rigidly formal were as alien to the former's concept of landscaping as the invention of form was to the latter's concept of architecture.

Alfred Caldwell chose trees, shrubs and other plants which were native to the region. He used them in a manner which subtly established scale, provided open or sheltered areas and screening, and which furthered the interpenetration of Mies van der Rohe's linked exterior spaces.

The interaction between this free-flowing landscaping, with its diaphanous honey locusts and substantial hawthorns, and the pristine architecture, contributes a kind of poetry to both exterior and interior milieu. Illinois Institute of Technology and Lafayette Park, in particular, show how effectively this 'natural' approach to landscaping may contribute with architecture towards the creation of a livable urban environment.

346. Illinois Institute of Technology.

347. Seagram Building, New York.

348. Crown Hall, Illinois Institute of Technology.

Urban Spaces—Summary

The preceding examples have illustrated the bearing Mies van der Rohe's structural and spatial concepts had upon the way in which he brought buildings together in urban environments. The following factors were largely responsible for the character of these projects.

(1) The evolution of a scale range spanning from the clear statement of a building's magnitude (through the expression of the structural system and the components of its construction) down to the building elements which confront the pedestrian, enables the buildings and the spaces to relate harmoniously with the human being.

(2) The insistence upon open ground floors for multi-storey buildings provides easy access, adds clarification to the structural system, sets a transitional scale between the exterior and interior spaces, and visually and physically opens up one street to another.

(3) The introduction of single-storey structures into plaza areas satisfies special space requirements, establishes an intermediate scale gradation between the pedestrian and the big space and provides the important element of visible human activity within a building at plaza level.

(4) The interpenetration of the exterior spaces gives identification to individual areas, while allowing the larger whole to be sensed. A natural approach to landscaping supplements and complements this interpenetration and brings spaces of different size towards a common equilibrium.

(5) Concern for the immediate visual and tactile experience of people is indicated by the use of the most direct solutions for entering buildings; and, by the careful selection and detailing of materials which stand up well under constant abuse for such items as plaza paving and steps, boundary walls and benches.

(6) By keeping the plaza spaces free of clutter, they have been able to accept many diverse activities for the entertainment and participation of the public.

These are all characteristic qualities of Mies van der Rohe's urban work and together they have enabled the buildings and the spaces between the buildings to contribute on equal terms towards the creation of a spatially varied, yet conceptually unified environment. An environment that is restrained and humane, at one and the same time, in scale with the city, its traffic and its people.

349. Toronto-Dominion Centre.

350. Concert on the plaza of the Toronto-Dominion Centre.

351. Lunch-time on the Toronto-Dominion Centre plaza.

352. Plaza level, Toronto-Dominion Centre.　▷

Education of Architects

Mies van der Rohe looked upon teaching as a great stimulant, because he was forced to clarify his ideas in order to be able to teach them. Moreover, teaching permitted him to work on general architectural problems; he knew from experience that there would not be adequate time to think about architecture when working on an actual building, the thinking had to be done before.

'The function of education', he said, 'is to lead us from irresponsible opinion to truly responsible judgement; and since a building is a work and not a notion, a method of work, a way of doing, should be the essence of architectural education.' But when he settled in Chicago in 1938 in order to direct the School of Architecture at Armour Institute, later to be merged with Lewis Institute to form Illinois Institute of Technology, he found that all the schools in the country were following the ideas of the Beaux Arts—a tradition for which he could find no justification whatsoever. He was convinced that a student should not be expected to design a building before he had assimilated the basic tools of his work. 'In the Beaux Arts Schools,' he said, 'first year students were already designing; I did not think this realistic, because a student must first have the basics—something on which he can stand. This is not a new idea, the master builders of the medieval times progressed from the craftsman level; they knew just about everything about the job of building by the time they became masters. Every student can be a good draftsman if he will work, and many can learn to be good constructors. But it is only one student, every year or two, whose discipline and experience entitle him to use his fantasy.'

The curriculum which Mies van der Rohe evolved for his school at I.I.T. and which continues to operate there embodied a philosophy of architecture and a method of architectural education that is not widely known or understood. Above all else he was determined that everything in his school should lead to reason—the curriculum had to depend upon and serve this philosophy. 'I believe that an architectural curriculum is a means of training and education,' he said; 'it is not a thing in itself, it depends upon and serves a philosophy. The absence of the philosophy is not a virtue, although some people think it is. It is a weakness not to have a philosophy. A curriculum without a philosophy is not broad and wide, not even neutral, but nebulous.

'It is my opinion that everything should be guided by reason—in order that one is kept on the right track. Some people do not think of reason in connection with architecture—they forget that a brick wall is a very reasonable affair. At our school we tried to develop a system of training and education in which everything leads to reason; I thought that if there were nothing in the course against reason, the student would attack everything with reason.'

The training aspect of Mies van der Rohe's curriculum is concerned with practical purpose; it deals with knowledge and skills, and makes clear, step by step, what is possible in construction, what is necessary for use, and what is significant as art.

The education aspect of the curriculum (which was never realized at I.I.T. to the degree Mies van der Rohe would have wished) is concerned with values; its purpose is to enable the training to be put to proper use through the understanding of science and technology, and the other significant forces which give shape to our epoch. Self-expression, in the normal sense, is not at a premium. The curriculum leads to a study of principles and, therefore, general rather than special solutions. The student undergoes a course of study in which each exercise forms a natural part of a consistent evolution, and as he is not called upon to discard or refute anything he has learned in previous years, he soon becomes cognizant with the continuity and the logical development of his studies.

When architectural educators asked Mies van der Rohe to define those decisions which he considered of prime importance for the direction of a school of architecture, he would often respond by saying that, first, it was essential to know what kind of school was wanted: 'This decision in itself will determine the quality of the school. The faculty should be as good as possible to maintain this direction, but even the finest group of talented men pushing in the wrong direction or in different directions means not only nothing, but, also, chaos. Architectural schools today are suffering from this lack of direction—not from a lack of enthusiasm, nor from the lack of talent. If we could only show the schools and faculties that individuality is inevitable and that it, too, has its natural place. To try to express individuality in architecture is a complete misunderstanding of the problem, and today most of our schools either intentionally or unintentionally let their students leave with the idea that to do a good building means a different building; and they are not different—they are just bad.

'I believe that in architecture you must deal with construction directly, you must, therefore, understand construction. When the structure is refined and when it becomes an expression of the essence of our time, it will then and only then become architecture. Every building has its position in a strata—every building is not a cathedral. These are facts which should be understood and taught. It takes discipline to restrain oneself. I have many times thought this or that would be a wonderful idea, only to overrule this impulse by a method of working and thinking. If our schools could get to the root of the problem and develop within the student a clear method of working we should have then given him a worthwhile five years. But five years is a very short time when you remember that in most cases these are the most formative years to the architect. At least two things should have been accomplished; mastery of the tools of his profession, and the development of a clear direction. Now it is quite impossible to accomplish the latter when the school itself is not clear.'

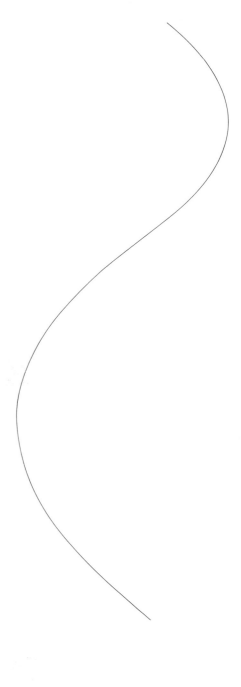

353. Drafting exercise (first-year student).

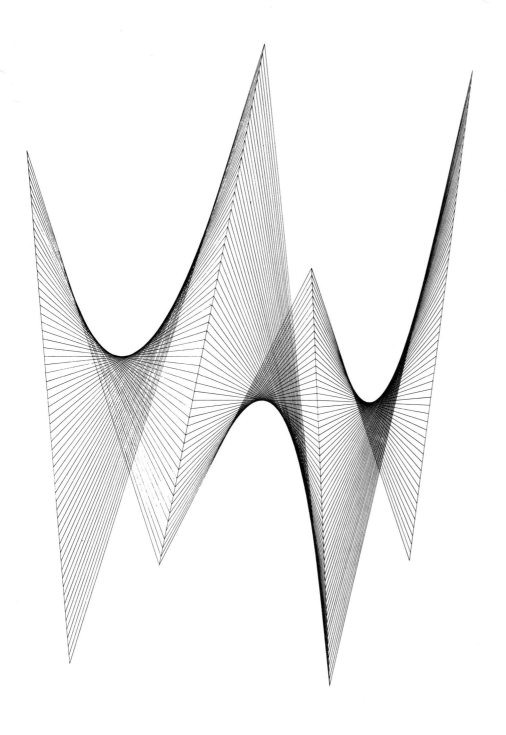

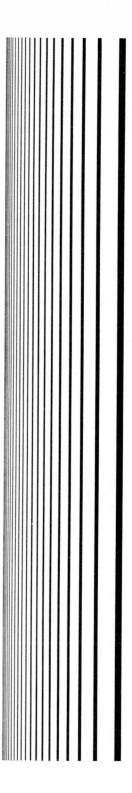

354. Drafting exercise (first-year student).

355. Drafting exercise (first-year student).

The following account of the curriculum of Mies van der Rohe's school at I.I.T. is based on an article by Professor R. F. Malcolmson, published in the Journal of Architectural Education, Autumn 1959, entitled 'A Curriculum of Ideas'.

Throughout the *first year* the student is preoccupied entirely with the tools and techniques of drawing. He learns the discipline of drawing well, with clarity and precision. These exercises are intended to give visual instruction in addition to displaying drafting dexterity.

The *second year* student learns basic construction in brick, wood and stone. He learns to understand their intrinsic properties and he uses his knowledge to make simple buildings. The construction exercises are complemented with courses in visual training comprising the study of form, proportion and rhythm, texture and colour, mass and space. These studies are abstract, not involved with building forms. They train the eye, and deal with the exigencies of materials on another level. The visual training aspects of the curriculum were initiated by the late Walter Peterhans.

In his *third year* the student extends his knowledge of construction to concrete and steel, while continuing with more advanced visual training problems. In addition, he now begins to study simple functions such as those of a bedroom, a bathroom and a kitchen, and relate these to houses of different sizes and types, later applying the same method of analysis to more complex buildings. He develops an ability to analyse a programme on a functional basis.

During the first three years of his studies the student has learned to draw well, knows basic construction, has studied proportion and space relations and begins to understand the function and planning of simple buildings. In the *fourth year* these separate aspects are brought together and further clarified through design problems involving simple buildings. The fourth year student is, also, introduced to the basic elements of town-planning with theoretical studies based on densities, land use and zoning and leading to an application of the principles discovered in a project for the replanning of an existing town. This aspect of the curriculum was initiated by the late Ludwig Hilberseimer.

In his *fifth-year* the student is offered an option in either architecture or town planning. This choice constitutes not only a final year of undergraduate studies but virtually an introduction to graduate work. Fifth-year architecture deals with advanced problems involving the expression of structure and materials, groups of buildings and their interrelationship and project studies. Fifth-year planning students undertake regional studies, the methods of survey and research and projects for the replanning of a region.

Courses in mathematics, basic mechanical and structural engineering and other technical as well as liberal arts studies are, also, taught during the undergraduate years. However, one of the most unusual and important aspects of Mies van der Rohe's curriculum is its unique teaching of the history of architecture. History is taught not only in the formal courses on this subject but there is, also, continual reference to historical examples in most of the other courses. The student studies history to understand the principles involved in the different building types of the past and in the architectural expression of past cultures. He is helped to understand the history of architecture, not to imitate it, for if he understands the cultural situations of the past he is better fitted to interpret the present. In this respect the lectures on architectural history which Alfred Caldwell delivered between 1950 and 1960 formed a cardinal part of the curriculum, parallel to and essential for its aims.

The school's *graduate programme* in architecture or city planning covers two years and since the students have varied backgrounds, coming from different areas in the United States as well as from abroad, the first year of their work is devoted to basic problems of an advanced nature so as to bring them to a common understanding for the second year's thesis project.

356. One of a series of construction exercises in which the student studies different structural solutions for a given plan.

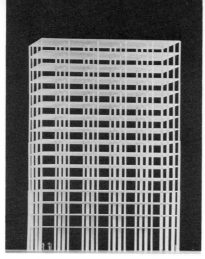 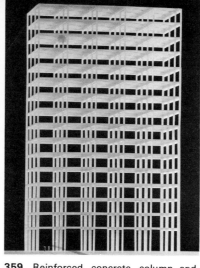 

358. Reinforced conc. flat slab; 16 stories.

359. Reinforced concrete column and beam structure; 16 stories.

360. Brick piers and reinforced concrete floor slabs.

361. Reinforced concrete; 14 stories.

362. Steel skeleton frame; 16 stories.

363. Steel frame; single storey.

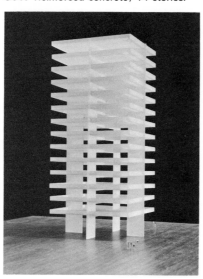   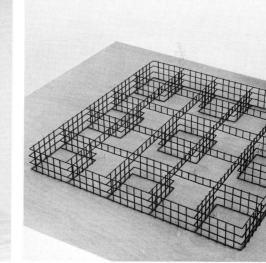

364. Student project for a residence using steel skeleton frame construction. The bedroom wing is separated from the living accommodation by the entrance lobby link.

365. In the court house exercise the student studies simple planning requirements and discovers their effect upon spatial relationships.

◁ **357.** An exercise in which the student studies various systems of enclosing simple steel and reinforced concrete skeleton framed buildings.

358–363. Structural studies of various magnitudes executed by students under the direction of Professor Alfred Caldwell.

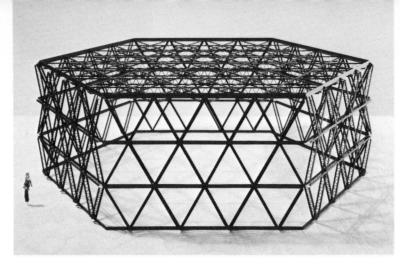

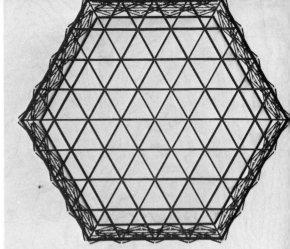

366–367. Steel bar joist.

368–369. Dome-steel.

370. Steel cable.

366–376. Advanced structural studies of various magnitudes executed by students under the direction of Professor Alfred Caldwell.

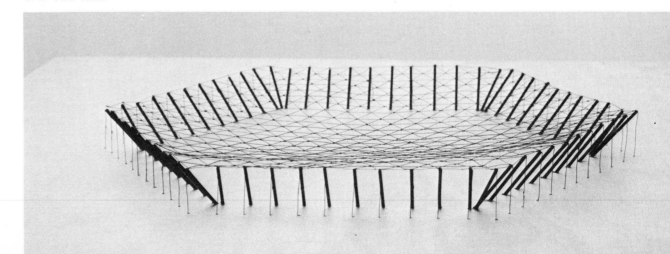

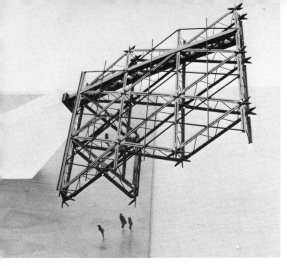

371–372. Steel bar truss vault—313 ft span.

373–374. Steel cable structure—10,000 ft span.

375–376. Steel structure—265 ft square.

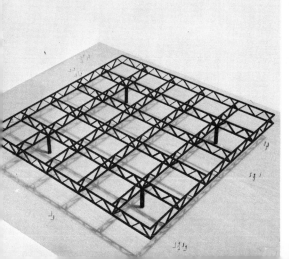

377. Graduate student project for a community building.

378 and 379. Graduate student project for an aeroplane hangar, executed under the direction of Professor Myron Goldsmith. (Each structural bay: 168 ft by 189 ft. Depth of main girder: 9 ft 6 in).

380. Graduate student space frame study. (240 ft by 240 ft, depth of structure 8 ft).

381 and 382. Graduate project for an exhibition hall, executed under the direction of Professor Myron Goldsmith.

383 and 384. Graduate student project for a sports arena, executed under the direction of Professor Myron Goldsmith. Bay size: 55 ft by 650 ft.

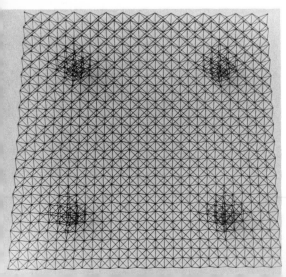

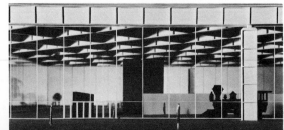

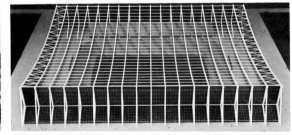

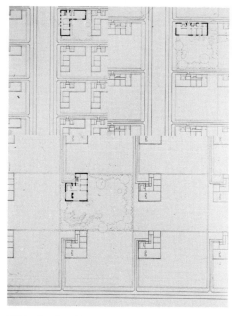

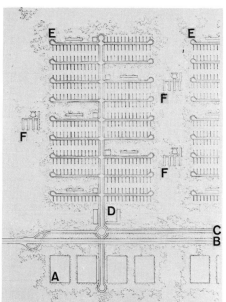

385. Studies illustrating the effect of different densities on the plans of houses.

386. Study for settlement unit. (a) Industry. (b) Highway. (c) Local highway. (d) Commercial. (e) Residential. (f) School.

387–390. Studies for replanning Elkhorn, Wis. **387.** Existing. **388.** First stage.

389. Second stage. **390.** Final stage.

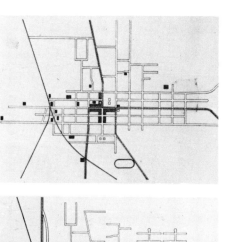

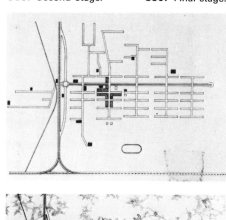

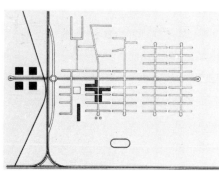

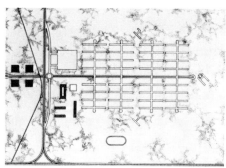

385–397. City planning studies executed under the direction of Professor Ludwig Hilberseimer.

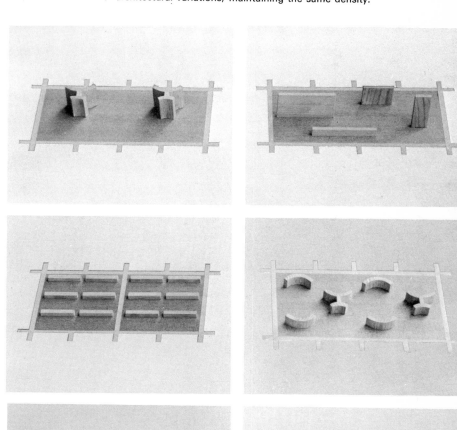

391. Housing development on the Fox River, Illinois. (High-rise apartments, houses, shopping centre and schools.)

392–397. Studies of architectural variations, maintaining the same density.

Conclusion

In his 'Discourses on Architecture', the nineteenth-century architect and theoretician Viollet-le-Duc pointed out that 'The more the artist reasons on his art, the more he tries to perfect the expression by which he would interpret his meaning, he is led to strengthen the original expression—to render it clearer.' There could hardly be a more apt description of the way in which Mies van der Rohe worked. 'Reason', he said quoting St. Thomas Aquinas, 'is the first principle of all human work.' Out of this belief Mies van der Rohe built a way of work which rejected open speculation on the grounds that it consumes. rather than directs, our energies. He chose instead to work within a context based on fact, and by so doing, to focus attention on objective and general rather than subjective and particular problems.

Reason governed every aspect of Mies van der Rohe's approach to architecture, and it is this consideration above all others that was responsible for the logical development of his ideas from one building to another and for the subsequent unity of the work as a whole.

The close relationship between architecture and civilization was a matter of deep interest to Mies van der Rohe. He took great pains, however, to clarify the differences as he recognized them between Civilization and Culture. Civilization he defined as 'the order in the material realm', while Culture he saw as being 'the harmonious expression of order in the spiritual realm'. He said that we speak of the Roman Civilization and the Greek Culture and that that was how he understood it.

He admitted that anthropologists look differently at these phenomena: 'For them *what is* is Civilization. I do not agree with this. I think that you can only talk about Civilization when you have order in the material world. To achieve this order there has to be a unity of action, and there cannot be a unity of action without a unity of creative thought. In this respect I am convinced of the need for clarity in both thought and action. Without clarity, there can be no understanding. And without understanding, there can be no direction, only confusion—which is where we find ourselves today. Today there is no order, not even in the material sphere; the chaos we have in the architectural field shows this quite clearly.

'The structure of a civilization is not easy to define because it is in part the past, in part the present, and in part the future. The past, by its very nature, we cannot change. The present we have to accept and should master. But the future is open—open for creative thought and action, and I believe that the real acceptance of the present will be the basis for the future.'

That architecture is an expression of the structure of civilization was a fundamental consideration of Mies van der Rohe's philosophy: 'Only a relation which touches the essence of the time can be real,' he said. 'This relation I like to call a truth relation. Truth in the sense of Thomas Aquinas, as the "Adequatio et rei intellectus"; or as we would express it in the language of today: truth is the significance of facts.'

Furthermore, Mies van der Rohe was of the opinion that between facts and ideas there exists a true relationship and that the challenge to human beings lies in the understanding of this relationship. 'The objective facts are given to use,' he said. 'We have science, we have technology, we have industrialization. All are accepted as part of progressive existence, the question is how to guide them in a direction that is beneficial to all of us.'

Because Mies van der Rohe believed that architecture can be nothing more than an expression of the objective facts, the recognition of their existence was, he felt, of prime importance. But, as he pointed out, 'to understand an epoch means to understand its essence and not everything that you see. What is important in an epoch is very difficult to find out because there is a very slow unfolding of the great form. The great form cannot be invented by you or me, but we are working on it without knowing it. And when this great form is fully understood, then the epoch is over, then there is something new.

'Some people think that you should always be doing something new, they ask for more and more novelty—not the essential things. The essential is what architecture is about, and we should not be afraid if that gets a little boring. I believe that architecture must develop out of the epoch—this was how the old architecture developed, each epoch did the most that it dared. Thus the Gothic developed out of the Romanesque; certainly the Gothic must have seemed strange at first, but it came out of the Romanesque.

'Architecture is an historical process, it has little or nothing to do with the invention of interesting forms or with personal whims. I believe that architecture belongs to the epoch, not to the individual. That, at its best, it touches and expresses the very innermost structure of the civilization from which it springs. Since I understand that, I would not be for fashion or individualism in architecture; in my opinion all individualism is a left over from the time when Luther said, "Here I stand." I would look for more profound principles. Since I know that we are under the influence of science and technology, I would ask myself what result comes from this fact—can we change it or can we not change it? And the answer to this question

gave me the direction which I followed. I have tried to make an architecture for a technological society; I have wanted to keep everything reasonable and clear—to have an architecture that anybody can do.'

Mies van der Rohe would certainly have agreed that his concept of architecture could be interpreted as being both conservative and radical without implying contradictory aims. Conservative, because its basic ingredients were the traditional principles of structural order, spatial relationship and proportion. Radical, because it accepted as prime determinants the significant driving and sustaining forces of our time—those of science, technology, industrialization and economy. Furthermore, in realization it was often sociologically radical in that we may sense, in the very humility of the spaces which his buildings offer, the acquisition of civilizing freedoms from wilful architectural control and anachronistic custom.

Throughout Mies van der Rohe's creative life the idea of *structure*—whether applied to civilization or to architecture—pervaded his thought and directed his action. And it was in the morphological interpretation of 'structure' that he recognized a sound principle upon which the architecture of our scientific and technological epoch might develop. Today technology provides architects with a wide range of choice, but the freedoms it brings are frequently interpreted as a licence for individualism of a most egregious kind. Mies van der Rohe concentrated on a structural architecture because he was convinced of its basis in reason, of its generality in application, and of its safeness as a way. 'If you do not follow this course you may go astray', he cautioned, 'and that would slow down architectural development or even make it impossible.'

An examination of Mies van der Rohe's work will reveal a gradual and consistent unfolding of structure as *Art*—within the context of the needs and means of our time. Although he was well aware that these needs and means would eventually give way to others, he was convinced that if the principle of structure remained secure, then the mainstream of architectural development would not be easily side tracked.

Mies van der Rohe's own buildings, the curriculum of his school and the work of many of his strongest students are tangible evidence of the practical application and validity of this concept. 'We are not at the end but at the beginning of an epoch.' He once said, 'the great historical epochs restricted themselves to very clear principles, yet they were certainly able to do anything; and I think that that is the only way you can make important architecture.'

398. Mies van der Rohe in Crown Hall.

Biographical   Notes

1886 The son of a master mason, Ludwig Mies van der Rohe was born in Aachen on 27 March 1886. The town of Aachen (Aix-la-Chapelle) is the oldest town on Germany's western border with the Netherlands; Charlemagne established the first capital of the Holy Roman Empire here and before its wartime devastation many buildings of the early Middle Ages attested to the town's previous eminence at the centre of western culture.

The medieval atmosphere of Aachen had a great impression on Mies van der Rohe: 'I remember seeing many old buildings in my home town when I was young. Few of them were important buildings. They were mostly very simple, but very clear; I was impressed by the strength of these buildings. They did not belong to any epoch; they had been there for a thousand years and were still impressive, and nothing could change that. All the great styles passed, but they were still there. They didn't lose anything and they were still as good as on the day they were built. They were medieval buildings, not with any special character, but they were really *built*.'

1905 Mies van der Rohe's formal education and subsequent technical training at a local trades school, where he gained a wide experience working as an apprentice on building sites, was followed by a period as a draftsman and designer of stucco ornament. In 1905 he was persuaded by an Aachen architect with whom he was then working to move to Berlin, then the centre of progressive architectural thought in the country.

1907 Two years later, when he was 21 years old, he followed an apprenticeship in furniture design with Bruno Paul by building a house for Dr. Riehl, a philosopher. A contemporary critic wrote that; 'The work is so faultless that no one would guess that it is the first independent work of a young architect.' The Riehl House was flavoured with the solid traditionalism of the vicinity. The form of the dormer window and the character of the roof came directly from local examples. It was, however, in the refinement of these elements together with the manner in which the house was placed on its steeply sloping site and in the whole interior treatment, including the furniture design, that a sense of quality was already evident.

Before allowing design work to proceed on his house Dr. Riehl had sent Mies van der Rohe to Italy for three months. On this trip Mies van der Rohe became very interested in the work of Palladio and Brunelleschi. In Florence he was particularly impressed by the Palazzo Pitti: 'A huge stone wall with windows cut out of it. And that is that. You see with how few means you can make architecture—and what an architecture!' In Rome he was impressed most of all by the Roman ruins, 'where no "architecture" was left but the structure'. The Basilica of Constantine was of great interest to him as were also the aquaducts: 'The aquaducts were all of the same character; the form changed only to suit the geographic situation, there was no regionalism involved.'

1909 After two years of independence Mies van der Rohe apprenticed himself in 1909 to Peter Behrens and, while in Behrens' office (where also were at one time Le Corbusier and Walter Gropius), he was put in charge of the construction of Behrens' German Embassy in St. Petersburg. 'Peter Behrens had a great sense of form. That was his main interest and that I certainly understood and learned from him.' Mies van der Rohe explained the apparent contradiction in Behrens' work as a typical phenomenon of the time: 'They found it natural to build factories in a modern way, but all representative buildings were in the classicistic expression. I think it must be very hard to break a tradition like that; it is a slow process.'

In Behrens' office Mies van der Rohe came under the influence of his master's great enthusiasm for the nineteenth-century German neo-classicist, Carl Friedrich Schinkel, the architect of a number of outstanding public buildings built in Berlin shortly after the Napoleonic wars. These works were distinguished by careful proportioning and by the articulated separation of the various architectural elements. While still working for Behrens, Mies van der Rohe built a house for Hugo Perls in which the spirit of Schinkel was prominent, as it was also in the Kroller House and to a lesser extent in the competition scheme for the Bismarck Monument, both of the following year.

Mies van der Rohe later commented upon the situation in Europe as he remembered it around this time: 'In Europe around 1900 a group of very talented men founded the Art Nouveau Movement. They tried to develop everything anew—houses, dresses, spoons, everything, even life, anew. They thought, however, that it was a question of form. The whole movement didn't last much longer than a typical fashion and nothing came out of it; yet they were most talented people; there were no finer in the world. It then became clear to me that it was not the task of architecture to invent form. I tried to understand what that task was. I asked Peter Behrens, but he could not give me an answer—he did not ask that question. Others said: "What we build is architecture", but we weren't satisfied with this answer; maybe they didn't understand the question. Since we knew that it was a question of the truth, we tried to find out what the truth really was. We were very delighted to find a definition of truth by St. Thomas Aquinas: *adequatio et rei intellectus* or as a modern philosopher expresses it, "Truth is the significance of fact". I never forgot this. It was very helpful and has been a guiding light. To find out what architecture really is took me fifty years—half a century.'

1910 The first European exhibition of the work of Frank Lloyd Wright took place in Berlin in 1910, at the same time as the publication of *Ausgefuhrte Bauten und Entwurfe* by Wasmuth. Mies van der Rohe studied Wright's work very carefully and found that it helped to clarify his ideas. Thirty years later he wrote the following appreciation for the unpublished catalogue of the Frank Lloyd Wright exhibition held at The Museum of Modern Art.

'The work of this great master presented an architectural world of unexpected force, clarity of language and disconcerting richness of form. Here, finally, was a master builder drawing upon the veritable fountainhead of architecture, who with true originality, lifted his creations into the light. Here again, at long last, genuine organic architecture flowered. The more we were absorbed in the study of these creations, the greater became our admiration for his incomparable talent, the boldness of his conceptions and the independence of his work invigorated a whole generation. His influence was strongly felt even when it was not actually visible.

'So after this first encounter we followed the development of this rare man with wakeful hearts. We watched with astonishment the exuberant unfolding of the gifts of one who had been endowed by nature with the most splendid talents. In his undiminishing power he resembles a giant tree in a wide landscape, which year after year, attains a more noble crown.'

1920 There was little actual building in Germany immediately following World War I. These quiet first years of the Weimar Republic were inductive to radical investigations of architecture's direction. It was the time of those experimental projects which collectively formed the polemic of the modern canon. By the early nineteen-twenties Mies van der Rohe's activities in Berlin had widened to include the direction of the architectural programme of the Novembergruppe, regular contributions to the magazine *G*, and a series of projects which included the designs for glass skyscrapers.

1924 At the time of these projects Mies van der Rohe made a forceful plea for the adoption of industrial methods in building. 'Our building methods today must be industrialized,' he wrote in the third issue of *G*, published in 1924. 'Although everyone concerned has opposed this until recently, it is now being discussed even outside the building trades. This seems like progress, even though few are yet really convinced.

'Industrialization, which is advancing in all fields today, would long ago have overtaken the building trades, in spite of their obsolete thinking, if there had not been special obstacles. I consider the industrialization of building methods the key problem of the day for architects and builders. Once we succeed in this, our social, economic, technical even artistic problems will be easy to solve. How can industrialization be carried out? The question can be answered if we consider what has thus far prevented it. Outmoded building methods are not to blame; they are the result rather than the cause.

'There have been many attempts to find new building methods which have succeeded only in those branches of the industry in which industrialization was possible. The potentialities of assembly methods in building have also been exaggerated; they are in use only in factory and barn construction. The steel industry pioneered the manufacture of fabricated parts ready for assembly, and today the lumber industry is trying the same thing. In all other building, however, the roughwork and most of the interior fittings are carried out in the traditional way by hand work. Hand work cannot be eliminated by changes in organization of the building industry, nor by improving work methods, for it is just this hand work that keeps small contractors going. It has been demonstrated that the use of larger masonry blocks can lower material and labour costs, but this in no way eliminates hand labour. Beside, the old brick masonry has many advantages over these newer methods.

'The problem before us is not the rationalization of the present methods, but rather a revolution in the whole nature of the building industry. The nature of the building process will not change as long as we employ essentially the same building materials, for they require hand labour. Industrialization of the processes of construction is a question of materials. Our first consideration, therefore, must be to find a new building material. Our technologists must and will succeed in inventing a material which can be industrially manufactured and processed and which will be weatherproof, soundproof and insulating. It must be a light material which not only permits but requires industrial production. All the parts will be made in a factory and the work at the site will consist only of assemblage, requiring extremely few man-hours. This will greatly reduce building costs. Then the new architecture will come into its own. I am convinced that traditional methods of construction will disappear. In case anyone regrets that the house of the future can no longer be made by hand workers, it should be borne in mind that the automobile is no longer manufactured by carriage-makers.'

1927 In 1927, as first Vice President of the Deutscher Werkbund, Mies van der Rohe organized the Weissenhofsiedlung Exhibition at Stuttgart, the purpose of which was to show the new ways of building houses and apartments.

Although he was commissioned as sole architect for the complete project, Mies van der Rohe decided to invite the foremost European architects to participate. Gropius, Le Corbusier, Oud, Stam, Behrens, Hilberseimer, Scharoun, Poelzig and Bruno and Max Taut, were among those represented, together with a number of local architects. The first project for Stuttgart was made in 1925 but was radically changed by the city's later decision to sell each house separately. Mies van der Rohe's own contribution to the Weissenhofsiedlung was a four-storey apartment building built around a steel skeleton.

After Stuttgart a period of exhibition and furniture design followed. Mies van der Rohe's exhibition designs were frequently made in collaboration with Lilly Reich. One of the exhibits on which they collaborated was made for the German Silk Industry in the 1927 Exposition de la Mode held in Berlin. Metal frames forming large flat or curved free-standing walls from which silk or velvets hung were disposed over a white linoleum floor. It was at this Berlin exhibit that Mies van der Rohe first used his MR steel furniture; he felt that upholstered pieces would have proved too heavy in this context.

1929 In 1929 Mies van der Rohe, associating with Lilly Reich, took charge of the German section of the International Exposition at Barcelona and designed a number of its exhibits, including the German Pavilion.

The following account of the Pavilion was written in 1929 by Nicolas M. Rubio Tuduri for Cahiers d'Art:

'It only contains space. It has neither a practical aim, nor a material function. People would say: "That's of no use." This is representative architecture, like an obelisk or an arch of triumph. Some architects, in order to represent Germany through some sort of a memorial structure, would probably have resorted to the form of, say, a great airship for this building. Mies van der Rohe, more discerningly, has given to his representative monument the serene form of a house.

'To be sure, there will not be an agreement on what exactly constitutes "the form of a house". When you build a true house, it remains a house no matter what you do to it. However, if you build something else which is not a house, yet want it to resemble one, it is necessary that you approximate your building to the well recognized forms of domestic architecture. Hence, a "traditional" element, a conservative aspect which we should not overlook, which indeed we find pronounced in Mies van der Rohe's Pavilion. Visitors and local citizens of the extreme *avant-garde* might perhaps take exception with him on this: "This pavilion is not the last word by any means." They are not too happy with the architect; they say it is not necessary to produce pseudo-novelties for International Expositions. But let me leave this judgement and return to my subject.

'The Pavilion only contains space, yet a space of a geometrical composition, not tangible, nor material. It has no doors, and furthermore, each room is only partially enclosed, by three partitions on three sides, for example. These partitions are, most of the time, made of large, continuous glass planes which confine the space only in a partial manner. Some of these glass planes are of sombre and neutral tint, reflecting people and other objects, and what you see through the glass mingles with what you see reflected on it. Some areas have no ceiling: these are true demi-patios where the space is defined only by three walls and the horizontal surface of water in a pool, yet where the space is "held" by the geometry.

'As you approach the Pavilion and then enter it, you are struck by this impression of non-utility which emanates from the open, empty rooms, from these beautiful walls of bare and unadorned marble, and from the patios not lived in; and you immediately feel the shock of, I dare say, metaphysical architecture. But I would like to pause here for a while in order to clarify this.

'The ordinary interpretation of the words "metaphysical architecture" would seem to be: architecture of the intellect, or of the intellectual abstraction. Everyone will understand when one wants to speak of proportions, of primary numbers, of clarity and near ferocity of the architectural reasoning, etc. In the German Pavilion of Barcelona, however, architecture gives way to evocation and symbolism, leaving reality behind. This is inevitable in representative architecture. During the speeches by the German delegates, one could not help saying something like: "Here is the spirit of the new Germany: directness and clarity of means and intentions—wide open to the breeze and full of sincerity— nothing will keep our hearts out. A mission honestly accomplished, without any conceit. Here indeed, the tranquil home of the appeased Germany!" This evocation has a markedly sentimental tendency: all the materials and even the geometry seem to give in to this feeling. It might appear surprising to discover something sentimental in a work of a very modern and very technical architecture; but we must recognize that architecture can hardly elude the social influences which give it its root.'

1930   Mies van der Rohe became director of the Bauhaus in 1930, but three years later he decided to close the school as a gesture against the Nazis. The background to the formation and dissolution of the Bauhaus may be summarized in the following way:

Germany's somewhat belated acceptance of the Industrial Revolution was followed from 1870 onwards by a complete reversal of attitude towards the new machine technology in a feverish attempt to level with England and France. So intensive was this effort that by the turn of the century the country found itself the leader of the industrial era. At this moment in German industrial development the influences of Ruskin and Morris began to be felt, influences which were soon to be given physical expression in such endeavours as the building of the Mathildenhoehe in Darmstadt and the foundation of the Kunstgewerbeschule in Weimar.

Henri van de Velde founded the Weimar Kunstgewerbeschule around 1902 on a philosophy based largely upon the English Arts and Crafts Movement (van de Velde had become an enthusiastic follower of William Morris during a stay in England in 1889 and he was presumably fully in sympathy with Morris' definition of art as 'the expression by man of his pleasure in labour'). Twelve years later a more constructive attitude towards the machine was introduced at Weimar by Walter Gropius when he became director of the combined Arts and Crafts School and the Academy of Fine Arts and founded the Staatliches Bauhaus Weimar. The synthesis of the art and craft and the art and technology philosophies arising from Gropius' curriculum (the industrial side of which received greater emphasis when the Bauhaus moved to Dessau) produced the most influential single source of industrial design of our time.

Gropius resigned from the directorship of the Bauhaus in 1928 in order to return to his private architectural practice. During the following two years the Bauhaus was the scene of much political agitation; by 1930 the situation warranted the introduction of a new direction. It was in an attempt to save the Bauhaus from disintegration altogether that Gropius and the Mayor of Dessau invited Mies van der Rohe to take over the school's direction.

Mies van der Rohe went to Dessau in 1930 but two years later, when the school was functioning normally again, pressures from outside began to be felt. The state of Dessau had turned Nazi and the activities of the Bauhaus were no longer free from political interference. Mies van der Rohe's only

alternative to closing the school altogether was to reorganize the whole establishment as a private institution and to move it to a more favourable environment in Berlin. Here, the Bauhaus, occupying an unused factory building and operating under increasing financial and political difficulties, was kept alive for one final year. By autumn 1933 the hopelessness of the situation had become all too apparent and Mies van der Rohe, with the full support of his faculty, decided to close the school.

Mies van der Rohe was often asked to speak of the circumstances which culminated in the closing of the Bauhaus; the following text was compiled from transcripts of Mies van der Rohe's discussions with students at The School of Design, North Carolina State College and The School of Architecture, Illinois Institute of Technology.

'The rise of the Nazi movement was not so sudden; it began at Dessau, and Dessau was among the first states to become Nazi by election. Soon after the Nazis came to power the mayor told me that they wanted to see what the Bauhaus was doing. They wanted an exhibition for criticism and the mayor suggested that I take a two week vacation! But I stayed because I wanted to see these people. Among them was Schulze-Neuburg, a highly honoured man in the Nazi movement who had written a series of books around 1900 under the title *Deutsche Kulturarbeiten*. They were books on cultural tendencies in general, about old buildings and about the factories ruining the country— sentimental, aesthetic, typical of the misunderstanding of his day. He wanted to save wonderful towns. You can only save wonderful towns by building good new ones.

'It was then that I knew the position to be absolutely hopeless. It was a political movement; it had nothing to do with reality and nothing to do with art. Then the City of Dessau decided to close the Bauhaus and the mayor, who loved the Bauhaus and wanted to help us, suggested that we take all the machinery, all the weaving looms, and just leave.

'I rented a factory in Berlin for three years at the cost of 27,000 marks, a lot of money in Germany at that time. The building was in a terrible condition, so we all started to work on it until it was all cleaned up and painted white. This was a solid, simple factory, hidden from view by a broken-down old wooden fence. I can assure you that there were many who, when they saw this fence, went home; but others came through and stayed.

'One morning, walking over the bridge from which you could see our building, I nearly died. Our wonderful building was surrounded by Gestapo. The officer in charge told me that they were searching for a secret printing press. They also said that they were investigating the documents of the founding of the Bauhaus. We opened everything for inspection, I was certain there was nothing there that could be misinterpreted. The investigation took hours.

'I then made an appointment to see Alfred Rosenberg. He was the philosopher of Nazi culture and head of the movement called Bund Deutsche Kultur. My friends thought me stupid to go, they were afraid that I would be killed. I talked with Rosenberg for an hour. My friends, Lilly Reich and Ludwig Hilberseimer, were sitting across the street in a cafe window so that they could see if I came out alone, or under guard.

'During the meeting I told Rosenberg that the Gestapo had closed the Bauhaus and that I wanted it open again. I told him that the Bauhaus had a certain idea. This idea had nothing to do with politics. It had to do with technology. Then he told me about himself. He was a trained architect from the Baltic states, from Riga. "Then we certainly will understand each other," I said. "Never!" he said. "What do you expect me to do? You know that the

Bauhaus is supported by forces that are fighting our forces. It is one army against another." When I replied that I really didn't think it was quite like that, he said: "Why didn't you change the name when you moved the Bauhaus from Dessau to Berlin?" I said: "Don't you think the Bauhaus is a wonderful name? You cannot find a better one." He said: "I don't like what the Bauhaus is doing. I know that you can suspend and cantilever, but my feeling demands a support." "Even if it is cantilevered?" I said, and he said, "Yes." When he asked me what we wanted to do at the Bauhaus. I said, "Listen, you are sitting here in an important position, look at your writing table, this shabby writing table. Do you like it? I would throw it out the window. That is what we at the Bauhaus want to do. We want to have good objects so that we do not have to throw them out of the window." Then he said, "I will see what I can do for you."

'From then on I went every second day for three months to the headquarters of the Gestapo. I felt that I had to because my school was at stake. It took me exactly three months to get to the head of the Gestapo. He said, "Come in. What do you want." "I would like to talk to you about the Bauhaus," I said. "What is going on? You have closed the school. It is my private property, and I want to know for what reason you have closed it. We didn't steal anything. We didn't make a revolution." "Oh," he said, "I am very interested in the Bauhaus movement, but we are not sure about Kandinsky." I told him that I would make all the guarantees for Kandinsky. "You have to," he said, "but be careful; we don't know anything about him, and if something happens, we pick you up." He was very clear about that. And then he said: "I will talk with Goering, because I am interested in this school."

'When I finally got a letter saying that we could open the Bauhaus again we ordered champagne and I called the faculty together: Albers, Kandinsky, Hilberseimer, Peterhans and others, and I said: "Here is the letter from the Gestapo, we can open the Bauhaus again." They said: "That is wonderful." I said: "Now, I went to the Gestapo headquarters every second day for three months just to get this letter. I was anxious to get this letter because I wanted to have the permission to go ahead. And now I make a proposition, and I hope you will agree with me. I will send a telegram to the Gestapo saying, "Thank you very much for the permission to open the school again, but the faculty has decided to close it!" I had planned this moment; everybody accepted it and was delighted. That was the end of the Bauhaus.'

1938 Mies van der Rohe had received his first invitation to settle in America as early as 1935 when the architect John Holabird proposed his taking over the Architectural Department of Chicago's Armour Institute; but he was not, at this time, in the mood to leave Germany. A year or so later, however, he visited America at the invitation of Mrs. Stanley B. Resor, the wife of the president of the Walter Thompson Advertising Company, to inspect a site at Jackson Hole, Wyoming, where the Resors intended to build a house. Work on this design was delayed until Mies van der Rohe settled in Chicago in 1938.

On the return trip from Jackson Hole, Mies van der Rohe took the opportunity of calling upon President Heald of the Armour Institute and Mr. Holabird in Chicago, and the invitation to take over the Architectural Department of the Institute was again proposed. Although working in Germany was becoming more and more difficult, Mies van der Rohe's acceptance of President Heald's offer was conditional to his being given a completely free hand in the reorganization of the school, together with the inclusion on his staff of two former associates from the Bauhaus—Professors Ludwig Hilberseimer and Walter Peterhans.

In 1938 Mies van der Rohe was formally appointed Director of Architecture at Armour Institute (in 1940 Armour Institute joined with Lewis Institute to form Illinois Institute of Technology), a position he retained until the pressure of a constantly expanding architectural practice forced his retirement from teaching in 1958. While he was associated with I.I.T. he undertook the preparation of a master plan for its new campus and subsequently designed many of its buildings.

1948 The construction of Mies van der Rohe's first American apartment building, Promontory Apartments in 1949, initiated a unique and prolific association with the developer Herbert S. Greenwald, in whose idealism Mies van der Rohe acknowledged 'the ability of convincing skeptical financiers that our buildings could and should be built'.

Greenwald's idealism inevitably made him impatient with the slow progress of urban redevelopment and his own efforts to rectify this condition quickly put him amongst America's foremost developers for the Federal Government's Urban Renewal programme.

'Herbert Greenwald began with an idea of the social consequences of his work', Mies van der Rohe said, 'along the way he also discovered that he was a very good business man.' But although this was certainly true, Greenwald always remained sincerely dedicated to his civic responsibilities and his loyalty to Mies van der Rohe was unshakeable. (On one occasion he turned town $12 million for the projected Commonwealth and Esplanade apartment groups from a financier who demanded various modifications to the design.)

Herbert Greenwald was 29 years old when he approached Mies van der Rohe for the Promontory building; thirteen years later he was killed in an air crash. 860 Lake Shore Drive; Commonwealth Promenade; Pavilion and Colonnade in Newark; the 1,800 dwelling redevelopments of Lafayette Park in downtown Detroit; and many other schemes were by then either built or under construction: making a lasting and unique contribution to urban living.

1950 On 17 April 1950, Mies van der Rohe delivered the following address at the Blackstone Hotel, Chicago, in which he discussed the relationship of Technology to Architecture:

'Technology is rooted in the past. It dominates the present and tends into the future. It is a real historical movement—one of the great movements which shape and represent their epoch. It can be compared only with the classic discovery of man as a person, the Roman will to power, and the religious movement of the Middle Ages.

'Technology is far more than a method, it is a world in itself. As a method it is superior in almost every respect. But only where it is left to itself as in gigantic structures of engineering, there technology reveals its true nature. There it is evident that it is not only a useful means, that it is something, something in itself, something that has a meaning and a powerful form—so powerful in fact, that it is not easy to name it. Is that still technology or is it architecture? And that may be the reason why some people are convinced that architecture will be outmoded and replaced by technology. Such a conviction is not based on clear thinking. The opposite happens. Whenever technology reaches its real fulfilment, it transcends into architecture. It is true that architecture depends on facts, but its real field of activity is in the realm of significance, I hope you will understand that architecture has nothing to do with the inventions of forms. It is not a playground for children, young or old.

'Architecture is the real battle ground of the spirit. Architecture wrote the history of the epochs and gave them their names. Architecture depends on its time. It is the crystallization of its inner structure, the slow unfolding of its form. That is the reason why technology and architecture are so closely related. Our real hope is that they grow together, that some day the one will be the expression of the other. Only then will we have an architecture worthy of its name: Architecture as a true symbol of our time.'

1950 Honorary Doctor of Engineering, Institute of Technology, Karlsruhe, Germany.

1954 The manner by which Mies van der Rohe was selected as architect for the Seagram company's headquarters in New York City is described in the following article by Phyllis Lambert entitled 'How a Building Gets Built'; this account was originally published in the Vassar Alumnae Magazine of February, 1959.

'*Post War Building.* The new buildings that mushroomed with the post war boom in New York were a dismal lot. Demand for office space was tremendous and office buildings moved up town to Park Avenue. No thought was given to the meaning of a city nor to the men who lived in it. With the need for more space, the old zoning law which regulated the height and placement of buildings on Park Avenue was broken. Instead of rising 20 stories clean from the street, the new structures were allowed to zigzag back, with a tower 25% the size of the property sticking up out of a wedding cake base. Buildings were no longer really built; rather full-scale models of set-back zoning laws appeared, covered by cheap metal and glass curtain walls.

'But a building cannot be ignored as a painting can be passed by, or a book left unread. It imposes itself on us, for we must approach it, find our way into it and through it, be enveloped by it. It is a visual and kinetic experience. As we approach a building, we are aware of its size and mass. Our eye is delighted or repelled by the proportions of the whole, its parts, its details. We are conscious of the materials we pass and step on, the space the building creates inside and out. These spatial intangibles, as well as the materials and detailing, have a direct influence on human beings, for we have a reaction to them, conscious or not.

'The responsibility for superior planning and painstaking detail required to make a building pleasing to the eye and spirit, and eminently habitable, would appear to fall solely on the architect. But the moment business organizations and institutions decide to build, they claim responsibility and take a moral position; and upon the choice of architect depends the quality of the statement.

'Usually these institutions, occupied with their own business, are content to have a real estate developer take over these infinitely complicated building problems and affix their name to the resulting skyscraper. If they do not buy a ready-made package, how are they to choose the architect? In the middle fifties the few masters of modern architecture were generally unknown. Modern architecture was viewed with suspicion if considered at all. With one or two exceptions the new ziggurats were being designed by hugh architectural firms who, thanks to their stereotyped thinking, were the undisputed leaders in the number of square feet built.

'In 1954 Joseph E. Seagram and Sons at last decided to build on Park Avenue. I was living in Europe when Seagram's intent to build reached me in Paris in July through a rendering of a very mediocre building. I flew to New York and started to learn all I could about the good buildings built since the war, and I consulted with architectural critics. I felt that my task was to explain to my father, the president of the company, what the business's responsibility could mean in terms of architecture and to convince him of the validity of the new architectural thinking that started to mature in the twenties.

'*My Architectural Research.* My father could not leave the choice of an architect to me without making sure that my attack made sense and that the architects of whom I spoke had the experience to build a skyscraper. He consulted a friend, Lou Crandall, the head of a large construction firm. By the middle of August, my real work began. I wrote to Eve Borsook:

' "Now I really have a job. I shall be travelling all over . . . Crandall wants me to do the research, the talking to the architects, etc. He told my father that I could do a job that no one else could have done, going to these people and talking to them. Certainly no one employed by Seagram could (by virtue of being employed), and a daughter who is interested in seeing that her father puts up a fine building seems to have everyone's sympathy.

'Through Marie Alexander (V.C. '44) at the Museum of Modern Art, I met Philip Johnson who was then the Chairman of the Department of Architecture. Through him and Mr. Crandall I was to meet and talk to the leading architects, the heads of the architectural schools, the architectural historians and critics (among them, Aline Bernstein Saarinen '35), the editors and writers of art and architectural magazines and the members of museum staffs.

'It was most important to see the recent buildings. In New York were the United Nations Building and Lever House. Outside of New York there were a fair number of buildings. Eero Saarinen's auditorium and chapel at M.I.T. were in construction, Gropius' Harvard Graduate Center was recently finished, and The Architects Collaborative had built houses and schools nearby. In Connecticut, there were houses and a small office building for Schlumberger by Philip Johnson and also houses by Breuer. Philadelphia was still proud of the PSFS by Howe and Lescaze built in the early thirties, an object lesson in the quality of interior detailing. In Philadelphia there was also the psychiatric wing of the Jewish Hospital by Lou Kahn and there was his Museum at Yale University. One could see Harrison's ALCOA building in Pittsburgh and his auditorium for Oberlin University. In Detroit, were Eero Saarinen's General Motors complex, Yamasaki's addition to a Bank building, and in the surrounding country a school by Yamasaki and a library by Breuer. I. M. Pei's Mile High Center was in construction in Denver. Chicago, the wealthiest American city architecturally, now had Mies van der Rohe's Twin Towers at 860 Lake Shore Drive and his growing campus at I.I.T. In Racine, Wisconsin, there was Frank Lloyd Wright's Johnson Wax Tower.

'*Choosing the Architect.* While looking at the buildings and talking to those concerned with architecture, the question to be asked was obviously not who should be the architect, but who was now going to make the greatest contribution to architecture? Were the masters of the 20's still leading the way or were the younger men, the second generation?

'In the two and a half months of searching, it became clearer and clearer that it was Mies van der Rohe who had so understood his epoch that he had made poetry of technology. In his 1950 address to the Illinois Institute of Technology Mies had said: "Wherever technology reaches its real fulfilment, it transcends into architecture." Through superb detailing and clarifying and articulating the structural system, Mies has given it artistic expression and created a language and vocabulary of architecture.

'The October 30th letter makes obvious my choice of architect:

'It has been said that Frank Lloyd Wright was the greatest architect of the nineteenth century . . . To me the Johnson Wax is a complete statement of "Manifest Destiny", the embodiment of all the philosophy of that period in America. It has a force and vitality that is almost cyclonic. It's crazy as hell and as wonderful as it is crazy. The greatest errors of taste—not errors, just plain bad taste—turn out to be magnificent. . . . His is not the statement that is needed now. America has grown up a bit and Frank Lloyd Wright has expressed what it was when its energies were unharnessed. . . .

'Le Corbusier has not built a building in this country. (The UN was unfortunately only an emasculation of his plan.) Would he be a great and good influence here? I am afraid not. . . . One is fascinated by his spaces, his sculptural forms, but are not people likely to be blinded by these and skip over the surface only? Mies forces you in. You have to go deeper. You might think this austere strength, this ugly beauty, is terribly severe. It is, and yet all the more beauty in it.

'The younger men, the second generation, are talking in terms of Mies or denying him. They talk of new forms—articulating the skin of façades to get a play of light and shadow. But Mies has said, "Form is not the aim of our work, but only the result." In his Farnsworth house in 1951 and the Twin Towers at 860 Lake Shore Drive in Chicago in 1952, he has articulated the skin, at the same time creating a play of depth and shadow by the use of the basic structural steel member, the I beam. This ingenious and deceptively simple solution is comparable to the use of the Greek orders and the Flying Buttress. It is not a capricious solution; it is the essence of the problem of modern architecture that Mies had stated in 1922: "We should develop the new forms from the very nature of the new problems."'

'At the beginning of November, my father asked Mies van der Rohe to be the architect of the Seagram building. Mies asked Philip Johnson to join him. On consultation with Mr. Crandall, our working force was set up. The associate architects who would produce the working drawings, the engineers and the rental agents were chosen.

'It was an unusual team that produced an unusual building. My father placed his trust and confidence in his architect, and in Mr. Crandall who was not only in charge of construction, but who was to help determine and watch costs. Mr. Crandall and I became, virtually, the clients. On leaving Paris, I had not intended to do more than help, choose the architect and then return, but it became increasingly clear to me that the person who had chosen the architect must stay with the job to fight for the concept.

'The Owner stated his requirements to the architect: The building was to have roughly half a million square feet of usable office space. Clients almost invariably present their architects with endless ideas they have dreamt of and reams of efficiency charts and studies prepared by a hierarchy of committees. Instead my father simply told Mies that his building was to be the crowning glory of everyone's work—his own, Crandall's and Mies'. And so began four fascinating years of work.

'*Planning the Building.* Letter to E.B.—1 December 1954.

'I have been named Director of Planning so that everyone will have to go through one central person.

'Three weeks ago, the contracts were signed and Mies came up—he and Philip found offices. Then the architects offices (where I will work) had to be installed, and then they got to work. Mies wanted the facts and the problems began.

'The first facts were the zoning laws—and the first problem, the air rights. According to the zoning laws, a tower can cover only 25% of the plot. Seagram intended to demolish only 375 Park Avenue, now the Montana apartment house, but with the area of 375 alone, we would have an unworkable tower, only 8,000 square feet gross. It is much too small for everything. However, Seagram also owns some land behind 375—116 East 53rd Street and two smaller buildings on 52nd Street. We could enlarge our tower if we could borrow the air rights to these buildings, but we find we can't unless they are included as a part of the new building, i.e. converted to offices, for they are apartment houses. So in a meeting in Crandall's office, we looked again at 116 and the small houses facing it on 52nd—(someone long ago had said oh let's not pull them down and the question stayed there) and we discovered that it was ridiculous to leave them as they do not make financial sense anyway. So the night after the meeting I called my father and told him we had just pulled a couple of buildings down for him—et voila! But still more problems—now we

have to get the people out of these buildings so that we can begin demolition. . . .

'NOW TO THE BUILDING—what can we do without a wedding cake (buildings that set back from the street in layers until they get to the tower)? There are three solutions. First, a square tower—which is out. Second, a 7:3 rectangular building set at a right angle to Park Avenue, the solution of Lever House. The third solution, set a 5:3 rectangular building back 90 feet from Park Avenue, creating a PIAZZA. The apartment houses mentioned above are to be rebuilt and form the background for the tower. They will be connected somehow and so your first six floors will have huge floor space and there will be a terrace garden and interesting shapes on top of the six-story building.

'Later, we bought a 100×100 foot plot on 52nd Street rounding out the site to 200×300 feet. This allowed for a still larger tower. Mies enlarged the tower by adding a one-by-three bay spine to its east face, and this spine formed the connection to the six-story east wing.

'Guess what solution will be picked? Mies hasn't said which yet, but he is only thinking in terms of the last one. There will also have to be STEPS leading to the Piazza as there is a big drop (8 feet) from Park to Lexington and you can't have a building with columns of different heights marching down the hill, and so it has been placed on a podium.

'This solution for the building has promise for terrific things—set back you hardly see it from the street coming up or down the Avenue *but* now what an impression—when you arrive there—almost Baroque, you don't know what is there and then you come upon IT—with a magnificent plaza and the building not zooming up in front of your nose so that you can't see it, only be oppressed by it and have to cross the street to really look at it, *but a magnificent* entrance to a *magnificent* building all in front of you—How excited I get just thinking of it—Oh how right the decision of Mies is—I become more convinced every day . . .

'*My Job.* As the basic requirements for the building were being determined in consultation with the rental agents and the mechanical and structural engineers, more and more information was gathered. One had constantly to work with the manufacturers, to re-examine production techniques and products. This was true of the bronze, the glass, the air conditioning units and enclosures, the lighting system and fixtures, the elevator cabs, the plumbing fixtures, the Venetian blinds—the list could go on and on. We are still working on many of these problems in the design of the restaurant in the east wing.

'The letters I have quoted indicate some of the complications of planning and the multitude of facts that must be gathered and collated. But information required for a building, like information required for a thesis or a balance sheet, can amount to jabberwock talk. A good building depends on the clarification and ordering of information by the artistic volition, and on the freedom of the framework in which the architect can work. My job was to make sure of this freedom and to avoid the rankling lack of understanding and short-sighted compromise that have atrophied or killed too many buildings.

'The finished building reveals the clarity of approach which gives it meaning both as an individual creation and as part of the city. It indicates too, I think, what a city could become if only vision were implemented by the devotion of all concerned.'

1955 Honorary Doctor of Engineering, Technological Institute, Braunschweig, Germany.

1956 Honorary Degree of Doctor of Laws, The University of North Carolina.

Elected Member of the German Order Pour Le Merite.

Professor Emeritus of Architecture, Illinois Institute of Technology.

Commander's Cross of the German Order of Merit.

Gold Medal of the Royal Institute of British Architects.

While in London to receive the R.I.B.A. Gold Medal, Mies van der Rohe was interviewed by the architect and city planner, Graeme Shankland for the BBC Third Programme:

Graeme Shankland: Mies van der Rohe is the most powerful intellectual influence in contemporary architecture. No other architect in this century has sought more deeply to discover what should be first principles in architecture today and none has worked more logically and systematically to develop and purify the architectural concepts built on these principles. His studies of glass towers represent a continuous development, from his first projects for Berlin in the nineteen-twenties, to the Lake Shore Drive Apartments in Chicago and the new Seagram Building in New York. He works in the spirit of a scientist seeking discoveries which will then have an objective value transcending the personal judgements which have created them.

In all this he differs sharply from the other three men who have decisively shaped world architecture in this century, Wright, Aalto and Corbusier. A more different personality from that of Corbusier it would be difficult to imagine. While Corbusier has illuminated architecture and the world around us with a brilliant display of his own rockets, Mies has been more like a lighthouse, shedding a clear, continuous beam—with each sweep burning with a more powerful and revealing force. When he came to Britain this year to receive the R.I.B.A.'s Gold Medal, its highest honour, he was preceded by his reputation as a kind of architectural delphic oracle—unapproachable, taciturn and cryptic.

I found that he was none of these things. He has measured the value of his achievement, and equipped with sharp senses of humour and discrimination, is without false pride. He is in love with logic, but also in love with his own buildings as expressions of it; and he is a master-craftsman who relishes sensuously his skill in handling materials and structure. Mies' claim on history, as I see it, is of one who brings quality to the inevitable. Like Milton, he is a poet of the clear and reasonable.

In this conversation we started by discussing his life-time search for architectural order. We went on to examine whether open planning is a liberation or a tyranny and how prefabrication should be approached if it is not to be a tyranny. Finally Mies speaks about the projects he still hopes to build and we return, via the question of the city, to his architectural philosophy. As an illustration of one kind of architectural order he takes the example of one of his buildings, the Architects' building in the campus of the Illinois Institute of Technology. This consists of one vast hall, supported on a basement and free of internal columns and fixed partitions, its roof hung from four deep and exquisitely detailed bare, black steel girders which stand up clear of the roof, outside the building. It is sheathed from floor to ceiling in glass. The whole campus, the buildings and the spaces between them, is planned on a grid, and I put it to him that this was an example of his search for a kind of order as a guiding and directing force.

Mies van der Rohe: You have to realize there are different stages of order. The real order is what St. Augustine said about the disposition of equal and unequal things according to their nature. That is real order. If you compare the Architects' building with the other campus buildings you can see that. When I put a grid over the whole campus, that was a mechanical help. No one had to speculate where we put our columns. We put our columns on the crossing

points of the grid all the way through. In the Architects' building I went away from the grid; I took just the grid in a larger measure but the elements are not in the grid any more. The grid was twenty-four feet apart. I think the Architects' building is the most complete and the most refined building and the most simple building. In the other buildings there is more a practical order on a more economical level and in the Architects' building it is a more spiritual order.

Shankland: This more fundamental idea of St. Augustine's, how has it helped your work, and your designing?

Mies: I would not build a church as a movie palace and I would not build a factory as a church, so we may a clear distinction what the value of these buildings are. There is not only a hierarchy of values, there is a hierarchy of works too.

Shankland: But, at the same time, on a gramophone record which you made a few years ago I heard you say that there should be the same kind of language for a garage as for a cathedral. How do you distinguish between these things?

Mies: We use the same principles, just as the Gothic men used the same principles for a cathedral as they would use for a barn. And that is what I meant by that.

Shankland: Your own work has had a big influence all over the world, in Europe and in America. How do you see the results on the work of other architects?

Mies: I think the influence my work has on other people is based on its reasonableness. Everybody can use it without being a copyist, because it is quite objective, and I think if I find something objective I will use it. It does not matter who did it.

Shankland: Mies not only discards what he discovers to be illogical or confused but severely limits the types of building structure he explores, isolating those he considers most important, like the multi-storied glass tower and the single-storey glass hall, and subjecting these to an uncompromising aesthetic discipline in the search for the clearest possible architectural expression. To use his own words: 'We intentionally restrict ourselves to those structures which are possible at the moment and try to work them out in all the details. In this way we want to create a basis for further development.'

He can do this because for him architecture is structure and as such not something to be played about with. Neither is it a question of just selecting a convenient or economic structure, then leaving it to the structural engineers to work out. He approaches architecture in the same spirit as the successive designers of the Gothic cathedrals, who worked for 300 years to perfect one type of structure. I asked him how he worked with his structural engineers. As I expected, he said that mostly he had to tell them what to do.

Mies: There are some structural engineers, you wouldn't have to tell them—in fact, they go their way alone. But the others know how to figure things out but they do not know the meaning of the work, so we have to say what structure is; they know nothing about structure, they know everything about construction.

Shankland: It seems to me and must seem to many people, I think, that there are not many different ways in which one could live in one of your houses. Even the way the furniture is arranged is something which flows directly from the plan of the buildings, and the open planning principles do impose a certain way of living in a house. Could you tell us how you came to this idea of the open plan? Does it, for instance, have any relation with the ideas of Mondrian and the aesthetic ideas of painters like him?

Mies: No, it does not: I think that was a mistake that the Museum of Modern Art made. They interpret it this way. But that is nothing to do with it. I never make a painting when I want to build a house. We like to draw our plans carefully and that is why they were taken as a kind of painting.

Biographical notes continued on page 181

Shankland: But none the less the open planning idea which you and Frank Lloyd Wright and many architects since have adopted is an aesthetic idea.

Mies: Certainly, yes.

Shankland: There have been criticisms, by people who live in this country in open planned houses, that they do not find them convenient, that they are draughty and they have no privacy: that kind of thing.

Mies: Yes? I would not like to live in a cubical house with a lot of small rooms. I would rather live on a bench in Hyde Park.

Shankland: What kind of house, if you were designing one for yourself, would you design?

Mies: I would build a simple but very large house, so that I can do inside what I like.

Shankland: You would like to change things round occasionally, as the Japanese do in their houses?

Mies: Yes, something like that.

Shankland: There have been criticisms of modern architects that they are seeking to impose a way of life, a way of living, particularly in houses, particularly through open planning, on the people.

Mies: Yes? We do not do that. We use the principle of flexibility. For instance in one of our tall buildings on Lake Shore Drive, Chicago, there are 400 apartments in the building and I cannot remember that two apartments were similar. We cannot help but fix the bathrooms and the kitchens in one place, but otherwise it is quite flexible, we can take the walls out or put more walls in.

Shankland: So that you regard open planning in this context as a liberating thing?

Mies: Oh, certainly. And the flexibility is in my opinion a vital necessity—for instance in office buildings.

Shankland: The most perfect small house you have built is the Farnsworth house; it is a classic example of the open plan—a single space glazed on all four sides, free of partitions, and only a service core with bathrooms, kitchen and mechanical equipment rising to the ceiling in the centre. Was this not an aesthetic idea imposed on a reluctant client? The Italian critic, Bruno Zevi, had said that this was not a house at all—but a museum.

Mies: No, that is not a fact. It was a house for a single person; this makes the problem more simple. I made later a house with five bedrooms and five bathrooms and even help quarters in glass. That is really a difficult problem, to make an open plan, but it is possible: you have to work only much harder on it. No, the Farnsworth house is, I think, not really understood. I was in the house from morning to evening. I did not know how colourful nature really was. But you have to be careful in the inside to use neutral colours, because you have the colours outside. These always change and I would say it is beautiful.

Shankland: And you had raw silk curtains, I think, in the same house.

Mies: Yes, and a very neutral primavera wood; and the whole floor of the house was Roman travertine, including the kitchen, bathrooms, and the terrace.

Shankland: That is why, I think, you painted the columns white?

Mies: Yes: That was the right colour in the country, you know, against the green. And I like black too, particularly for cities. Even in our tall glass buildings, when you are in an apartment, you see the sky, and even the city, changing every hour. I think that is really new in our concept.

Shankland: Here, not only does Mies reject the suggestion that the open plan can be a tyranny, but he claims for it not just the practical advantages of flexibility but a more important spiritual one of setting the scene for a 'really new' and profound relationship between man and nature in town and country.

I then took up with him the question of prefabrication. In a modern industrial society based on factory production, every serious architect has to make up his mind on what terms he approaches this question. In his own work, Mies has always used the individual products of modern industry, but never designed completely prefabricated buildings. I asked him why this was.

Mies: I do not think it is an advantage to build planned prefabricated houses. I think the value of prefabrication is the value of getting elements which we can use freely as we have doors and bath tubs. We have many other buildings. In our steel buildings we have about 3,000 windows and only two shapes. I think that is the best way of prefabrication. To prefabricate a house or standardize a house from top to bottom is too complicated a process. So I think it is much better that industry should deliver elements which we can use in a free way. Otherwise it would be terribly boring. And I do not think it will happen.

Shankland: At the same time there has been in Europe, on a very wide scale now, and in Germany and Russia this use of this *grossen Plattenbau*—I think they call it—system: 'large plate-building', or the use of systems of construction involving an entire wall being placed into position by a crane, and so forth. But that does not seem to have interested you. You think this is a limiting factor on an architect, this kind of thing?

Mies: Yes, and I think it is not right. When I can build a skeleton where I have really thin columns and they are much stronger than these heavy walls, I would rather use a skeleton and put glass in it, a light material again. Glass is the best material. I have had the chance of drinking wine out of glasses 2,000 years old. They were in the ground and nothing had happened; they were discoloured a little, but they were otherwise perfect.

Shankland: This moving tribute to glass reminded me that Mies came to building first as a craftsman, apprenticed in his father's stone-cutting shop in Aachen. He has not forgotten his first-hand impact with materials but transcenced it in an ability to extract the last drip of character from every material he uses. The Seagram Building, New York's latest skyscraper, in its luxurious purity and calm authority makes all earlier ones seem clumsy or, at best, pretty. It also represents the culmination of forty years of intense study of glass towers, of ideas which first took preliminary shape in Europe but which, rejected in Nazi Germany, could be realized only in America. I asked him what other projects and ideas he still hoped to realize as a man of seventy-three.

Mies: I am not a business man, but an architect. And there is not much I would like to build. Perhaps a Convention Hall I designed for Chicago, and some other things, maybe a house for myself.

Shankland: I think you had news today of a new job?

Mies: That is a Federal Court building in Chicago. It has many court-rooms and is a complicated building. We have even to put a prison on the top of it. I am curious what comes of it.

Shankland: Apart from that, which is an actual commission, what buildings would you still now particularly like to do that you have not so far done?

Mies: I would like to build one of these huge halls we designed. I do not know if you remember the design for the Convention Hall in Chicago? It was 720 feet by 720 feet without any support inside. And the Bacardi building for Cuba is 65 metres by 65 metres without any support inside. The President of Bacardi wanted just one large room for his whole office.

Shankland: Finally we turned to the question nearest to my own heart as an architect-planner, to the city; first to the only project in town planning as a co-ordinating exercise he has ever realized, the Weissenhofsiedlung in Stuttgart in 1927. Here he conceived a three-dimensional master plan to guide a collective demonstration of what contemporary architecture could do to produce an environment for a whole community, and invited sixteen leading modern architects to design individual buildings. Did he regret not having had an opportunity to do this kind of thing in America?

Mies: It was an ordeal to do it in Stuttgart, and I can imagine it would be more difficult in America. I do not see the necessity to repeat things like that. In Stuttgart that was a certain hour in history that we could show at once that all these forces were at work but never visible really, and that was the reason we wanted to build this Weissenhofsiedlung, to show at once clearly that there is a new way of building houses and apartment buildings.

Shankland: What about the future of the Metropolis? Many people, as you know, are throwing up their hands in despair today, saying that it has no future. What is your view on that?

Mies: I think we are just at the beginning of changing the cities, but not in a romantic way. I am sure that the economic situation will have a great influence on the way our cities will be. I do not believe that we architects can just plan a city out of the blue sky. There are economic forces so strong we cannot change them. They can be guided, that is about all.

Shankland: When Mies' own career began he and his contemporaries had to break away from Art Nouveau. They found at hand in Berlin the neo-classical buildings of Schinkel built some eighty years earlier.

Mies: Around 1910, Schinkel was still really the greatest representative in Berlin; Das Alte Museum in Berlin was a beautiful building—you could learn everything in architecture from it—and I tried to do that.

Shankland: Did you find in Schinkel's work certain key leading ideas or approach which you have found useful since?

Mies: In the Alte Museum he has separated the windows very clearly, he separated the elements, the columns and the walls and the ceiling, and I think that is still visible in my later buildings.

Shankland: Finally we spoke of the moral idea that a building ought to express its structure. This central idea of the modern monument is expressed in Mies' buildings more than those of any other architect—but it derives from men like Ruskin and Viollet-le-Duc who practised something very different. Mies points to this paradox.

Mies: But Ruskin had quite romantic ideas about art. He said, you know, every decoration should be thrown out when it does not support the construction, and look what he did himself. It is very strange that somebody can have a clear idea and work in a different way, because he is the son of his time.

Shankland: But you are the son of yours in the sense that you have based your work on this scientific and objective and rational approach, helped by the philosophers whom you have been mentioning.

Mies: Yes, but I learned most from old buildings.

Shankland: Because they were scientific and rational too?

Mies: No, but they were clear and reasonable.

1960 Gold Medal of The American Institute of Architects.

Honorary Degree of Doctor of Fine Arts, Carnegie Institute of Technology.

Mies van der Rohe delivered the following address on the occasion of the presentation to him of The American Institute of Architects' Gold Medal at the annual convention held in San Francisco, April, 1960.

'To receive the Gold Medal of the American Institute of Architects is indeed a great honour. It is a sign that my work has been understood and appreciated by my colleagues. I am very grateful and very thankful for this distinguished token of esteem.

'May I also express, on this occasion, the deep gratitude I have always felt, and shall always feel, that I could come to this country and have the opportunity to teach and to work here. The teaching forced me to clarify my architectural ideas. The work made it possible to test their validity. Teaching and working have convinced me, above all, of the need for clarity in thought and action. Without clarity, there can be no understanding. And without understanding, there can be no direction—only confusion. Sometimes it is even a confusion of great men, like the time around 1900 when Wright, Berlage, Behrens, Olbrich, Loos and Van de Velde were all at work, each taking a different direction.

'I have been asked many times by students, architects and interested laymen: "Where do we go from here?" Certainly it is not necessary nor possible to invent a new kind of architecture every Monday morning. We are not at the end, but at the beginning of an epoch. An epoch which will be guided by a new spirit, which will be driven by new forces, new technological, sociological and economic forces. And which will have new tools and new materials. For this reason, we will have a new architecture.

'But the future comes not by itself. Only if we do our work in the right way will it make a good foundation for the future.

'In all these years I have learned more and more that architecture is not a play with forms. I have come to understand the close relationship between architecture and civilization. I have learned that architecture must stem from the sustaining and driving forces of civilization. And that it can be, at its best, an expression of the innermost structure of its time.

'The structure of civilization is not simple, being in part the past, in part the present, and in part the future. It is difficult to define and to understand. Nothing of the past can be changed, by its very nature. The present has to be accepted, and should be mastered. But the future is open—open for creative thought and action.

'This is the structure from which architecture emerges. It follows, then, that architecture should be related to only the most significant forces in the civilization. Only a relationship which touches the essence of the time can be real. This relation I like to call a truth relation. Truth in the sense of Thomas Aquinas, as the "Adequatio et rei intellectus". Or, as a modern philosopher expressed it in the language of today: "Truth is the significance of facts". Only such a relation is able to embrace the complex nature of civilization. Only so, will architecture be involved in the evolution of civilization. And only so, will it express the slow unfolding of its form.

'This has been, and will be, the task of architecture. A difficult task, to be sure.

'But Spinoza has taught us that great things are never easy. They are as difficult as they are rare.'

1961 Honorary Degree of Doctor of Humanities, Wayne State University.

Television station W.T.T.W. Chicago produced four programmes in which George Danforth interviewed Mies van der Rohe about his life and work.

1963 Gold Medal for Architecture, National Institute of Arts and Letters.

Honorary Degree of Doctor of Fine Arts, Northwestern University.

United States Presidential Medal of Freedom.

1964 Honorary Degree of Doctor of Fine Arts, University of Illinois.

1968 During October an exhibition of Mies van der Rohe and Lord Holford's Mansion House Square development generated a great deal of public interest in London (page 130). In the following article entitled 'Mies in the London Jungle' published in *The Spectator* issue of 1 November 1968, the architectural critic, Stephen Gardiner, assessed the scheme:

'So we are to have at last—touch wood—a building by Mies van der Rohe in the City. On show at the Royal Exchange the other day, 30,000 people saw his design for a single tower which will stand in a new square opposite Mansion House. We are very lucky indeed that Rudolph Palumbo had the courage to commission Mies for the work—we could do with more patrons like him. For

Mies is the last surviving member of the famous trio which changed the direction of architecture in his century. He has demonstrated in America how the tower should be designed and now he is to do so over here. He is the accepted master of this form and he shows us, and his commercial followers, that it is really a reasonably simple problem; and that it has to be treated as such, without all the silly embellishments of different materials for panels and structure and so on that in the end add up to no more than fussy, irrelevant and, often enough, horrible decoration.

'The Fine Art Commission has, of course, raised objections about the height of the building and its proximity to St. Paul's. I find this extraordinary. For one thing, the tower is a considerable distance away and the two buildings will, therefore, rarely be seen together; secondly, the cathedral has already been spoilt by frightful office blocks immediately around it which destroy both close-up views and those from across the river. And to go to the other extreme—from the sublime to the entirely ridiculous, so to speak—the relatively new St. Paul's Choir School, attached to the little tower of St. Augustine by Wren, ruins all kinds of angles from ground level in a way that Mies' design never could from half a mile away.

'It seems a great pity that the Fine Art Commission do not spend as much time discussing architecture as they do worrying about heights and diagrammatic planning schemes. Architecture is just as important and in some ways a good deal more so. After all, we don't normally see cities in panoramic views, and not often enough from above—or for long enough—to matter. Down on the ground, in London and particularly at the centre, one is far more concerned with individual situations, street scenes on a limited but massive scale, and there the detail of actual elevations to buildings is a vital part of what we see. To this, of course, the Commission would say that at least they help to get the broader issues right (although whether they do or not is open to question); certainly this should be true where they are dealing with open spaces such as the river, parks, countryside and so on. Nevertheless the fact remains that this is only a small part of the battle and it really doesn't matter all that much about shape and height if the building is in any case hideous. What we then see is an ugly elevation and we see it all the time, and for the rest of our lives.

'The visual responsibility of an architect is vast—this can never be emphasized too strongly—and the damage he can do is also vast. Mistakes are irrevocable; this is the big difference between architecture and other arts. A bad book can go on a shelf, a painting under a bed and even a Moore can be shifted with a crane, but nothing can be done about a building. Once it's there you're stuck with it. And as the building enlarges, so, obviously, does the architect's responsibility: there's far more to see, for one thing. Without doubt his most dangerous weapon is the tower, whether offices or flats or hotels. With a tower he can smash any beautiful building in the vicinity, and on an open site, like the Hilton on the edge of the Park, shorten distances that originally appeared infinite to a mere half-mile. Again, one wouldn't mind the Hilton nearly so much if it were good to look at. In fact, it is no worse and no better than innumerable other awful towers. One simply has to conclude that architects are too small to handle big buildings. They seem, for instance, unable to see their tower as the city object it is, getting bogged down instead on a much more domestic level with detail. They seldom assess the proportion correctly and usually end up with something thick and blunt. And they are utterly nonplussed by the junction of a tall vertical element with flat ground, blurring this inevitable happening with a confusion of self-deceptions—projecting wings, low blocks and so on—that make architectural impossibilities.

'On all these counts, Mies does precisely what was expected of him in the City, arriving at a simplicity that not even he has achieved before. The front of the Seagram Building in New York, for instance, conceals a certain bulki-

ness of plan, but nothing is hidden behind this pure structure that is 290 ft high, standing aloof and alone at the end of its square. It is made of only two materials, glass and bronze, and its proportion, based on a 13 ft floor height and a 6 ft 6 in module, is equally economical and direct. The entrance at street level is largely open and the tower lands on the ground with no fuss at all, a brief glass hall making the connection. Surprisingly, it doesn't seem particularly tall but this, I think, is because it makes no pretentious claims for itself; Mies' new tower possesses that calm and remote authority which does not dominate a space but peacefully occupies it. Like all good architecture, it seems to have happened quite naturally, almost by chance.

'That is by no means all. The magic goes on working. There is the new square, conjured out of the disappearance of the New Zealand Bank and a change in direction of Queen Victoria Street, and beneath it a shopping centre by the same architect. At any time one longs for more open space in cities—small gardens, a bit of green, some trees—because it lets blue sky into narrow streets, and here we have it, lighting up three forgotten buildings; St. Stephen's Church by Wren, the side of Mansion House, a bank by Lutyens. Suddenly—amazingly—something has been put right, the jungle has been cut down: a piece of *real* town planning has been done and stands a pretty good chance of being carried out: what on earth is going on in England? The answer is easy: the architect is Mies van der Rohe and he has insisted that, in three simple moves, order can be made out of chaos. The buildings which have been "discovered" in retirement may not be stars—and the post-war Bucklersbury block on the south side is, of course, beastly—but it's clear, even from the model, that this sparkling new tower by Mies will, by its sheer reticence, rub a new shine into the best of them.

'The height of the structure is right. Detail sizes are sufficiently small to equal those of the surroundings. A lifetime of experience has gone into it. How dare the Fine Art Commission disrupt the composure of such a beautiful thing when buildings like the Stock Exchange are allowed? Its members should concentrate on stopping stuff of little merit instead of permitting their supersensitivity to spoil the work of a great architect.'

1968 An hour-long television programme titled *The Master Builder* surveyed Mies van der Rohe's work with his participation.

1969 New National Gallery was completed in Berlin—60 years after Mies van der Rohe's first work, the Riehl House, was built in the same city.

17 August Mies van der Rohe died.

On 25 October James Johnson Sweeney, a long time friend of Mies van der Rohe, delivered the following tribute:

'Standing here in Crown Hall, with its scale that so appealed to Mies, I like to remember the first time I saw Mies van der Rohe and the impressions I had. It was in the Spring of 1933. I had admired an apartment interior he had designed for Philip Johnson who had recently settled in New York. I was on my way to Europe and Germany on a business trip. Philip Johnson suggested that I call on Mies. I wrote him. He invited me to his office. When my wife and I entered, we both saw at once the answer to a question which had been troubling us for some time: Why was the Barcelona seat so wide? As we opened the door we realized. Mies was seated on one and it just comfortably accommodated his breadth.

'Perhaps "amply" would be a more accurate word than comfortably. For we recognized something ample about Mies himself at that first glimpse—a quality which seemed related to everything about him, everything he admired, everything he did. The suit he was wearing was ample—well cut to be sure, but easy on him—and of a sober rich material. The cigars he offered me, and smoked one after another, were likewise "ample"—and of the finest Havana leaf. The glass and chromium steel table near which he was seated, which we had always thought strangely high in proportion to its width, now looked perfectly in scale with its designer. Even on the first visit, I realized Mies' love of space, scale and quality of material.

'And thirty-three years later I was reminded of that first sight of Mies, when one evening after museum hours, looking for him, I happened into his Cullinan Hall of the Museum of Fine Arts in Houston and found him alone in that sparsely hung, white gallery—100 feet by 95 feet with a ceiling 32 feet high—once again on a Barcelona seat, again smoking a similar cigar, quietly studying that space he had so sensitively proportioned.

Another incident I like to remember was a telephone call I made to Mies in his apartment on East Pearson Street before rushing off to a plane. I had been in Chicago for the day for a lecture and was on my way back to New York. In my apologies for not having reached him earlier I mentioned something of the general subject of my talk, order and form in contemporary painting. "Ah—yes," he said slowly, "Saint Augustine." Nothing more.

'Again I recall one Saturday afternoon in New York, happening to drop in at the Nierendorf Gallery. An exhibition was scheduled to be on view. To my surprise I found the gallery dismantled—or, rather, in the process of being dismantled. Mies was in town. And frequently he and his friend Karl Nierendorf used to take advantage of the weekend to clear the gallery walls of what was on view and amuse themselves in arranging a special exhibition of whatever they liked particularly, or wanted to see together from Nierendorf's stock. It might be a large selection of Nierendorf's best Paul Klees, of his *Die Brücke* pictures, or a single painting on a large, otherwise empty wall, a mode of presentation which particularly appealed to Mies.

'Mies enjoyed this. He found it one of the happiest ways to spend a quiet weekend in New York. He loved Klee's paintings as he had liked Klee personally. He knew, perhaps better than anyone else, how to choose a Klee painting of quality. And it was from Nierendorf's stock that he built up the excellent group of Klees he had in his East Pearson Street apartment—Klees, Schwitters, and, what was always a surprise, a large Beckmann nude in his bedroom!

'One has only to think of Mies' handsome 1942 drawing—and collage designs for "an ideal museum for a small city" to realize how much he enjoyed paintings and sculpture and his respect for them. In these projects one is hardly aware of the architecture. Where the presentation of works of art was concerned he felt that they should have complete priority. Architectural details, fantasies in installation or lighting that might even slightly distract the observer's attention from the works of art were inadmissible. The only features he permitted were open space and a sensibility in its division. The relative "absence of architecture", as he put it, intensifies the individuality of each work of art and at the same time incorporates it into the entire design.

'I remember his escape to New York ten days before the Cullinan Hall in Houston was inaugurated, distressed by the preparations for the first exhibition to be held there which he saw crowding the easy space he had envisaged for the hall. And I recall his request for photographs of an installation of the same gallery sometime later when only three large paintings by Miro were

hung, with a large Picasso oil and a monumental Chillida sculpture. He wanted to send it to Berlin with his project for the Berlin National Gallery. And he did so.

'Space, amplitude and a comfortable relationship among the parts—unity, order, form—were his basic requirements. A lack of order in any part hurt him.

'It is characteristic of the depth, complexity and subtlety of Mies' view of architecture that the man whose epicurean taste would wish to combine Roman travertine, Tinian marble, grey transparent glass, onyx and chromium-plated, steel columns in his Barcelona Pavilion and walls of striped black and pale brown Macassar ebony and tawny, gold and white onyx in his Tugendhat House could also declare with warmth and sincerity: "Where can we find greater structural clarity than in the wooden buildings of old? Where can we find such unity of material, construction and form?—What feeling for material and what power of expression there is in these buildings! What warmth and beauty they have! They seem to be echoes of old songs!" This from the Mies we associate with the statement that concrete, steel and glass are the materials of our time and from these materials the forms of our epoch should evolve! But for Mies everything depended on "how we use a material, not on the material itself—each material", as he said, "is only what we make it". And Mies, in no matter what material he employed, as the bequest of buildings he has left Chicago bears witness, was essentially a builder. He never forgot his early lessons from his master-mason father. "I learned about stone from him." And I recall how pleased he was to recount the fact that as a young man—barely more than a boy—he had qualified as a journeyman bricklayer. "Now a brick", as he would say, "that is really something. How sensible is this small, handy shape, so useful for every purpose! What logic in its bonding, pattern and texture! What richness in the simplest wall surface! But what discipline this material imposes!" On this homely basis Mies established an unparalleled expression of new materials and engineering techniques: "a form for an epoch". Discipline, order, form: this was the progress he saw underlying the statement from Saint Augustine he was so fond of quoting. This, for him, in architecture, was Truth. Beauty was its splendour.

'"All education", he felt, "must begin with the practical side of life", but "true education is concerned not only with practical goals but also with values. By our practical aims we are bound to the specific structure of our epoch. Our values, on the other hand, are rooted in the spiritual nature of man. Our practical aims measure only our material progress. The values we profess reveal the level of our culture—the long path from the material through function to creative work has only a single goal: to create order out of the desperate confusion of our time."

'And this is the bequest which Mies has left to all of us and particularly to Chicago: his vital, personal and inspiring patterns of order in a world which has suffered too long in recent years from the disregard of such a spiritual discipline.

'Today there is no need to stress the value of Mies' contribution, nor his stature as an artist. As the latter, he had the good fortune to live to realize the universal recognition that was being paid him. To the world he was a great architect and a modest, self-effacing man. To his intimates he will always remain, what he always was to them, a benign monolith: a warm friend and a full human being.'

Buildings and Projects by
Mies van der Rohe

(Numbers in parenthesis refer to chart)

399. New National Gallery, Berlin, Germany: 1962–8.

400. Riehl House, Berlin-Neubabelsberg, Germany: 1907.

Mies van der Rohe 1886–1969

Houses

Project: Mies van der Rohe Exhibit for V Bienal Exhibit, Sao Paulo, Brazil (129)

Project: Rockville Center Development (130)

1959–63 Project: Friedrich Krupp Administration Building, Essen, Germany (131)

1960–1 Project: Schaefer Museum, Schweinfurt, Germany (132)

1960–3 Home Federal Savings and Loan Association of Des Moines, Des Moines, Iowa
Associate Architects: Smith-Vorhees-Jensen (133)
One Charles Center, Office Building, Baltimore, Maryland (134)
2400 Lakeview Apartment Building, Chicago, Illinois
Associate Architects: Greenberg and Finfer (135)

Miscellaneous

1961 Project: Mountain Place, Montreal, Quebec (136)

1962–5 Social Service Administration Building, The University of Chicago, Chicago, Illinois (137)
Meredith Memorial Hall, Drake University, Des Moines, Iowa (138)

1962–8 New National Gallery, Berlin, Germany (139)
The Science Center, Duquesne University, Pittsburgh, Pennsylvania (140)

1963 Lafayette Towers, Lafayette Park, Detroit, Michigan (141)

1963–5 Highfield House, Apartment Building, Baltimore, Maryland (142)

High-rise buildings: offices

1963–9 Toronto-Dominion Centre, Toronto, Ontario
Mies van der Rohe, Consulting Architect (143)
John B. Parkin Associates and Bregman and Hamann, Architects

1965–8 Westmount Square, Montreal, Quebec
Resident Architects: Greenspoon, Freedlander, Plachta & Kryton (144)

1966 Project: Church Street South K-4 School, New Haven, Connecticut (145)
Project: New Haven, Connecticut Redevelopment (146)
Project: Foster City, Apartment Buildings, San Mateo, California (147)

High-rise buildings: apartments

1966–72 District of Columbia Public Library, Washington, D.C. (148)

1966–9 Project: Houston Museum Addition, Houston, Texas (149)
Project: Blue Cross Building, Chicago, Illinois (150)

1967–9 High Rise Apartment Building No. 1, Nuns' Island, Montreal, Quebec
Resident Architect: Philip Bobrow (151)
Project: King Broadcasting Studios, Seattle, Washington (152)

1967–8 Esso Service Station, Nuns' Island, Montreal, Quebec
Resident Architect: Paul LaPointe (153)

Low-rise buildings

1967–70 111 East Wacker Drive, Illinois Central Air Rights Development, Chicago, Illinois (154)

1967 Project: A New City Square and Office Tower, London, England
Joint Venture with William Holford and Partners (155)
I.B.M. Regional Office Building, Chicago, Illinois
Joint Venture with C. F. Murphy Associates (156)

Clear span buildings

1968 Project: Commerzbank AG, Office Building and Bank, Frankfurt/Main, Germany (157)

1968–9 High Rise Apartment Buildings No. 2 and 3, Nuns' Island, Montreal, Quebec
Resident Architect: Edgar Tornay (158)
Project: Northwest Plaza Project, Chicago, Illinois (159)
Project: Dominion Square Project, Montreal (160)

Urban spaces

1946–7	Project: Cantor House, Indianapolis, Indiana (73)
1946–9	Promontory Apartments, Chicago, Illinois Associate Architects: Pace Associates and Holsman, Holsman, Klekamp and Taylor (74)
1947	Central Vault, Illinois Institute of Technology, Chicago, Illinois (75) Project: Theatre (76) Project: Gymnasium and Swimming Pool, Illinois Institute of Technology, Chicago, Illinois (77)
1947–50	Institute of Gas Technology, Illinois Institute of Technology, Chicago, Illinois Associate Architects: Friedman, Alschuler and Sincere (78)
1948	Project: Student Union Building, Illinois Institute of Technology, Chicago, Illinois (79)
1948–50	Association of American Railroads Administration Building, Illinois Institute of Technology, Chicago, Illinois Associate Architects: Friedman, Alschuler and Sincere (80)
1948–51	860 and 880 Lake Shore Drive Apartments, Chicago, Illinois Associate Architects: Pace Associates and Holsman, Holsman, Klekamp and Taylor (81) Interior, The Arts Club of Chicago, Chicago, Illinois (82) Project: Algonquin Apartments, Chicago, Illinois (two versions) (83)
1948–53	Mechanical Engineering Building for the Association of American Railroads, Illinois Institute of Technology, Chicago, Illinois Associate Architects: Friedman, Alschuler and Sincere (84)
1949–50	Project: Cantor Commercial Center Office Building, Indianapolis, Indiana (85)
1949–52	Chapel, Illinois Institute of Technology, Chicago, Illinois (86)
1950	Project: Caine House, Winnetka, Illinois (87) Project: Dormitory and Fraternity Houses, Illinois Institute of Technology, Chicago, Illinois (88) Project: Chicago Beach Apartments, Chicago, Illinois (89)
1950–6	Crown Hall (Architecture, City Planning and Design Building), Illinois Institute of Technology, Chicago, Illinois Associate Architects: Pace Associates (90)
1950–1	Project: Steel Frame Prefabricated Row House (91) Project: Fifty Foot by Fifty Foot House (92)
1950–2	Mechanical Engineering Research Building I, Illinois Institute of Technology Research Institute, Chicago, Illinois Associate Architects: Friedman, Alschuler and Sincere (93) Project: Berke Office Building, Indianapolis, Indiana (94)
1951–2	McCormick House, Elmhurst, Illinois (95) Project: Pi Lamda Phi Fraternity House, Bloomington, Indiana (96)
1951–3	Carman Hall, Illinois Institute of Technology, Chicago, Illinois Associate Architects: Pace Associates (97)
1952–3	Commons Building, Illinois Institute of Technology, Chicago, Illinois Associate Architects: Friedman, Alschuler and Sincere (98) Project: National Theatre, Mannheim, Germany (99)
1952–5	Cunningham Hall, Illinois Institute of Technology, Chicago, Illinois Associate Architects: Pace Associates (100) Bailey Hall, Illinois Institute of Technology, Chicago, Illinois Associate Architects: Pace Associates (101)
1953–4	Project: Convention Hall, Chicago, Illinois (102)
1953–6	Commonwealth Promenade Apartments, Chicago, Illinois Associate Architects: Friedman, Alschuler and Sincere (103) 900 Esplanade Apartments, Chicago, Illinois Associate Architects: Friedman, Alschuler and Sincere (104)
1954	Master Plan for the Museum of Fine Arts, Houston, Texas (105) Project: Benseville Row Houses (106)
1954–8	Seagram Building, 375 Park Avenue, New York, New York In Association with Philip Johnson Associate Architects: Kahn and Jacobs (107) Cullinan Hall, The Museum of Fine Arts, Houston, Texas Associate Architects: Staub, Rather and Howze (108)
1955	Project: Lubin Apartment-Hotel, New York, New York (109)
1955–6	Master Plan for Lafayette Park, Housing Project, Detroit, Michigan. In association with Ludwig Hilberseimer (110)
1955–7	Association of American Railroads Laboratory Building, Illinois Institute of Technology, Chicago, Illinois Associate Architects: Friedman, Alschuler and Sincere (111) Physics-Electronics Research Building, Illinois Institute of Technology Research Institute, Chicago, Illinois Associate Architects: Naess & Murphy (112)
1956	Hyde Park Redevelopment, Chicago, Illinois (113)
1956–8	Metals Research Building, Illinois Institute of Technology Research Institute Associate Architects: Holabird and Root (114)
1957	Project: United States Consulate, Sao Paulo, Brazil (115) Project: Quadrangles Apartments, Brooklyn, New York (116) Project: Bacardi Office Building, Santiago de Cuba, Cuba (117) Project: Kaiser Office Building, Chicago, Illinois (118) Project: Commercial Building, Pratt Institute, Brooklyn, New York (119) Project: Pratt Institute Housing, Brooklyn, New York (120)
1957–8	Project: Battery Park Apartment Development, New York, New York (121)
1957–61	Bacardi Office Building, Mexico City, Mexico Associate Architects: Saenz-Cancio-Martin-Gutierrez (122)
1958	Pavilion Apartments, Lafayette Park, Detroit, Michigan (123) Town Houses, Lafayette Park, Detroit, Michigan (124)
1958–9	Project: Seagram Office Building, Chicago, Illinois (125)
1958–60	Pavilion Apartments and Colonnade Apartments, Colonnade Park, Newark, New Jersey (126)
1959–64	Chicago Federal Center, U.S. Courthouse and Federal Office Building Joint Venture: Schmidt, Garden & Erikson, Mies van der Rohe, C. F. Murphy Associates, and A. Epstein & Sons, Inc. (127)
1959	Chicago Federal Center, Federal Office Building and U.S. Post Office Joint Venture: Schmidt, Garden & Erikson, Mies van der Rohe, C. F. Murphy Associates, and A. Epstein & Sons, Inc. (128)

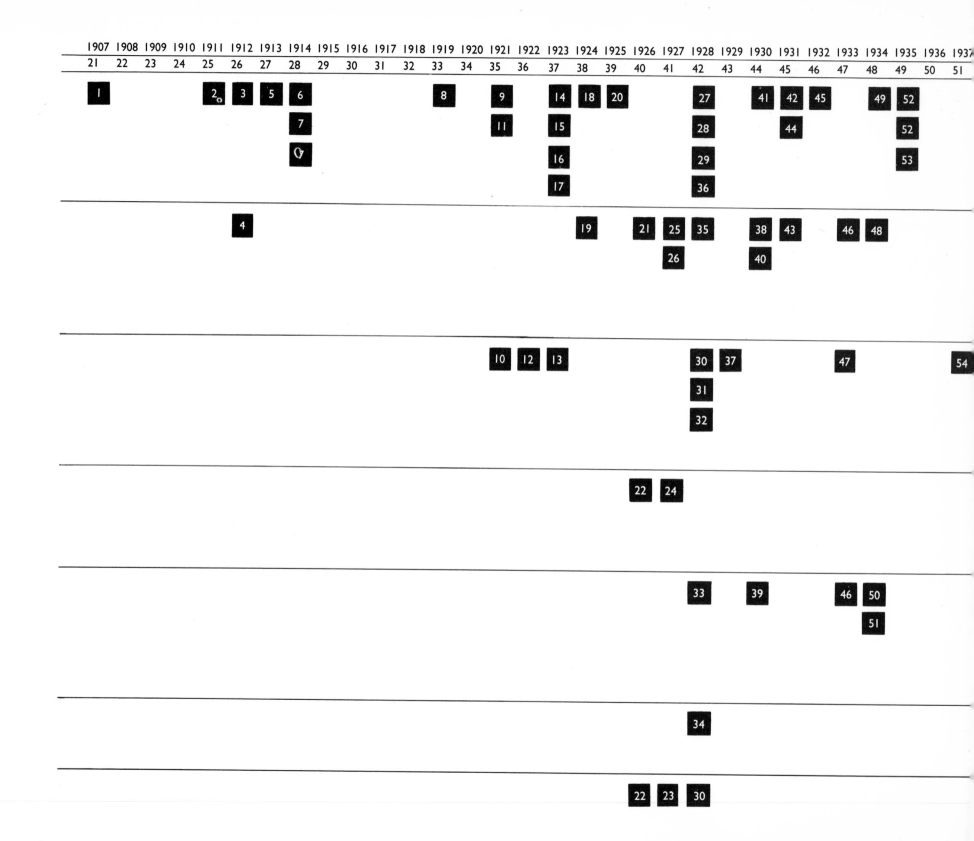

1938	1939	1940	1941	1942	1943	1944	1945	1946	1947	1948	1949	1950	1951	1952	1953	1954	1955	1956	1957	1958	1959	1960	1961	1962	1963	1964	1965	1966	1967	1968
52	53	54	55	56	57	58	59	60	61	62	63	64	65	66	67	68	69	70	71	72	73	74	75	76	77	78	79	80	81	82
55							71	73				87 91 92	95			106				124										
							64 65 66 72		75	82											129									
											85	94				107			118	125	128	134			143		144	150	152 154 155 156	157 159 160
								74		81 83		89	97	100 101	103 104		109		116 120 121	123 126 126		135		141 147			144	147	151	158 158
			58 60			61 62	63 67 68 69		78	79 80 84		88 93	96	98			111 112	114	115 119 122		128 131	133		137 138 140			144	145 148	153	
			59				70 71		76 77		86	90 92		99	102	105 108	117					132		139	143			149		
	56	57								81					103 104	107	110	113	121	126	127 130	133	136		143		144	146 147	155	159 160

Selected Bibliography

Blake, Peter, *Mies van der Rohe: Architecture and Structure*, New York, 1960

Blaser, Werner, *Mies van der Rohe—The Art of Structure*, Zurich, Stuttgart, London and New York 1965

Glaeser, Ludwig, *Ludwig Mies van der Rohe: Drawings in the Collection of The Museum of Modern Art*, New York 1969

Hilberseimer, Ludwig, *Mies van der Rohe*, Paul Theobald and Company, Chicago 1956

Hilberseimer, Ludwig, *Contemporary Architecture, Its Roots and Trends*, Paul Theobald and Company, Chicago 1964

Johnson, Philip C., *Mies van der Rohe*, The Museum of Modern Art, New York 1947

Acknowledgements

My first and deepest appreciation must go to Phyllis Lambert for her constant encouragement and constructive criticism, as well as for innumerable suggestions that contributed towards developing and refining the central thesis of this book.

I am also especially indebted to Sally Hasler for the careful preparation of the manuscript; to Anne Engel and Jean-Claude Peissel of The Pall Mall Press for their great assistance during the book's production phase; and to Eric Doel, David Needs and their colleagues at Butler and Tanner, Printers, for their patient co-operation during my visits to their press at Frome.

I should like to thank a number of people who have helped me in one way or another with my work on the book: Peyton Abbott, Professor Reyner Banham, Caroline Benn, Professor Daniel Brenner, Bruno Conterato, Professor George Danforth (who kindly permitted me to include examples of I.I.T. students' work), Joseph Fujikawa, Adrian Gale, Professor Myron Goldsmith, Godfrey Golzen, Jack and Ed Hedrich, Mary Anne Lea, Dirk Lohan, Paige Temple, Theresa Wallach, Suzie Watt, John Wolfers, Terry Young.

James Johnson Sweeney generously permitted me to print the full text of his moving tribute to Mies van der Rohe, given in Crown Hall on 25 October 1969 (page 183). Stephen Gardiner allowed me to include his article 'Mies in the London Jungle' which appeared in the *Spectator* issue of 1 November 1968; and George Gale, editor of the *Spectator*—the copyright holder—who also consented to its inclusion (page 182). Graeme Shankland and the British Broadcasting Corporation kindly agreed to my including 'Architect of the Clear and Reasonable', an interview of Mies van der Rohe by Mr. Shankland which was broadcast over the B.B.C. Third Programme and subsequently published in *The Listener* of 15 October 1959 (page 180). Phyllis Lambert and Mrs. John Van de Water (editor of *Vassar Quarterly*) permitted me to reprint the former's essay 'How a Building Gets Built', which appeared originally in the *Vassar Alumnae Magazine* of February 1959 (page 178). Dean R. F. Malcolmson allowed me to quote extensively from his article 'A Curriculum of Ideas' published in the *Journal of Architectural Education*, Autumn 1959 (page 162). Pao-Chi Chang kindly agreed to my including an abstract of the graduate team's report on the Chicago Convention Hall Project (page 102). E. G. Chandler, City Architect and Planning Officer, Corporation of London, generously reviewed my text 'A New City Square and Office Tower in the City of London'

(page 147). Extracts from 'The End of the Bauhaus' are reprinted by permission of the Student Publications of The School of Design, North Carolina State University, Raleigh, North Carolina—who hold the copyright (page 176).

The following writings and translations of writings by Mies van der Rohe are reprinted from 'Mies van der Rohe' by Philip C. Johnson, copyright The Museum of Modern Art, New York: 'Two Glass Skyscrapers' and 'The Office Building' (page 18); 'Frank Lloyd Wright—An appreciation written for the unpublished catalogue of the Frank Lloyd Wright Exhibition held at the Museum of Modern Art' (page 174); 'The Industrialization of Building Methods' (page 177).

Occasional sections of my text represent reworkings of material which previously appeared in: *Architectural Design*, London (March 1961); *Bauen & Wohnen*, Zurich (July 1961); *20th Century*, London (Spring 1964); *Architect's Year Book XI: The Pedestrian in the City*, Elek Books Limited, London 1965; *The Kentiku Journal of Architecture*, Tokyo (October 1969).

Whenever Mies van der Rohe is directly quoted in the text the source often derives from my own notes and tapes. Other sources include the rare speeches and interviews that Mies van der Rohe gave, and for making available to me transcripts of this material I am indebted to The Office of Mies van der Rohe; and also to Reynolds Aluminium, Richmond, Virginia for allowing me to quote from their record 'Conversations Regarding the Future of Architecture', copyright 1956, Reynolds Metals Company.

I wish to record a particular dept of gratitude to Dr. Ludwig Glaeser, Curator of the Mies van der Rohe Archive. The archive, which was established in 1968 at The Museum of Modern Art, New York, holds a vast amount of original material—including drawings, sketches and job correspondence—relating to the architect's work. Many of the illustrations in this book derive from this collection and some are published here for the first time.

Finally, and in addition to recording my obvious debt to the late Mies van der Rohe himself, I should also like to take this opportunity of mentioning the names of other people whose guidance and advice have helped me towards a clearer understanding of architecture in general and of Mies van der Rohe's work in particular: the late Professor Ludwig Hilberseimer, the late Professor Walter Peterhans, Professor Alfred Caldwell, Professor R. F. Malcolmson, the late Eero Saarinen, Gene Summers.

Catalogue of Illustrations

In this catalogue the illustration number is followed by the source and, when available, a photographer's negative number. Reprints not originated by the photographer listed as indicated by an asterisk*. Addresses of the photographers may be had upon request from the publisher. The author is indebted to all those persons and organizations listed for permission to publish the respective photographs for which they hold the copyright.

(1) Hedrich-Blessing 15412 A. (2) Hedrich-Blessing 17378 B. (3) Peter Carter. (4) Source unknown. (5) Combier. (6) Bill Engdahl, Hedrich-Blessing 18506 P3 Enl. (7) Peter Carter 262953–25. (8) Hedrich-Blessing 13809-Y4. (9) Chicago Architectural Photographing Company W-6280. (10) Hedrich-Blessing 32240. (11) Bill Engdahl, Hedrich-Blessing 18506 M. (12) Hedrich-Blessing 19452 E. (13) Bill Hedrich, Hedrich-Blessing 13809 L4. (14) Hube Henry, Hedrich-Blessing 14545 B. (15) Hedrich-Blessing 15412 E.* (16) Hedrich-Blessing 17356 E. (17) From a calotype print in the Victoria and Albert Museum, London. (18) Photograph from Phaidon Archives. Chromolithography from Dickinson's *Comprehensive Pictures of the Great Exhibition . . .* London, 1852. (19) Photo from Country Life. (20) Phyllis Lambert K10235-2/22. (21) Peter Carter 92026–10. (22) Peter Carter 262953–36. (23) Source unknown. (24–25) Zeitschrift des Vereines deutscher Ingenieure, LV, 30 Sept 1911. (26) Hedrich-Blessing 23097 F.* (27) Hedrich-Blessing 33370 D.* (28) Hedrich-Blessing 33370 S2.* (29) Williams and Meyer Company 60–7075–2.* (30) Hedrich-Blessing 27736 E. (31) Hedrich-Blessing 27736 E. (32) Hedrich-Blessing 10170 B. (33) Hedrich-Blessing 10170 B. (34) Hedrich-Blessing 23097 E.* (35) Hedrich-Blessing 23097 B.* (36) Hedrich-Blessing 33370 A.* (37) Hedrich-Blessing 26818 D.* (38) Hedrich-Blessing 17421 A.* (39) Hedrich-Blessing 9691 P.* (40) Hedrich-Blessing 23097 D.* (41) Williams & Meyer Co 9404 F.* (42) Hedrich-Blessing 30641 A.* (43) Hedrich-Blessing 33370 H2.* (44) Hedrich-Blessing 33370 C.* (45) Peter Carter. (46) Peter Carter. (47) Hedrich-Blessing 10170 C. (48) Hedrich-Blessing 10170 B. (49) Hedrich-Blessing 27736 C. (50) Hedrich-Blessing 9970 P. (51) Collection, The Museum of Modern Art, New York. Lenscraft 8810-3. (52) Collection, The Museum of Modern Art, New York. S 8293. (53) Hedrich-Blessing 9970 A2. (54) Collection, The Museum of Modern Art, New York. 88 47-3. (55) Collection, Mies van der Rohe Archive at the Museum of Modern Art, New York. MR 3232.18.5. (56) Collection, Mies van der Rohe Archive at the Museum of Modern Art, New York. MR 3232.18.9. (57) Collection, Mies van der Rohe Archive at the Museum of Modern Art, New York. MR 3232.18.1. (58) Collection, Mies van der Rohe Archive at the Museum of Modern Art, New York. MR 3232.18.6. (59) Collection, Mies van der Rohe Archive at the Museum of Modern Art, New York. MR 3232.18.3. (60) Peter Carter. (61) Hedrich-Blessing 3370 1.* (62) Hedrich-Blessing 15489. (63) Hedrich-Blessing 27736 B. (64) Bill Hedrich, Hedrich-Blessing 13809 L4. (65) Hedrich-Blessing 31899 F. (66) The Office of Mies van der Rohe. (67) Phyllis Lambert. Photograph reprinted by Hedrich-Blessing 34678. (68) Ron Vickers Ltd 16756 M 80. (69) Phyllis Lambert 114277–7. (70) Phyllis Lambert 114277–5. (71) Ron Vickers Ltd 16756 M 3. (72) Ron Vickers 16756 M 51. (73) Hedrich-Blessing 28647 B. (74) The Office of Mies van der Rohe. (75) Hube Henry, Hedrich-Blessing 28426 I. (76) Hube Henry, Hedrich-Blessing 28426 A. (77) Balthazar Korab 10357. (78) Hube Henry, Hedrich-Blessing 26587 A. (79–80) Peter Carter. (81–82) Peter Carter. (83) Hedrich-Blessing 12173 V. (84) Hube Henry, Hedrich-Blessing 28426 D. (85) Hedrich-Blessing 18837 X. (86) Hedrich-Blessing 18837 N. (87–90) The Office of Mies van der Rohe. (91) Hedrich-Blessing 13809 R4. (92) Harr, Hedrich-Blessing 31973 E. (93) Hedrich-Blessing 21451 F. (94) Hedrich-Blessing 21451 A. (95–99) The Office of Mies van der Rohe. (100) Ezra Stoller © ESTO 41 T 20. (101) Ron Vickers Ltd 16756 M 82. (102) Hedrich-Blessing 18837 L. (103) Hedrich-Blessing 18837 M. (104–106) The Office of Mies van der Rohe. (107) Bill Engdahl, Hedrich-Blessing 19715 B. (108) Sam Vandivert, Slant/Fin Radiator Corporation, Richmond Hill, New York. (109) Richard Nickel. (110) Ron Vickers Ltd 16756 M 80. (111) Hedrich-Blessing 13809 J5. (112) Hube Henry, Hedrich-Blessing 14545 B. (113) Peter Carter. (114) Hedrich-Blessing 15692 A. (115) Hedrich-Blessing 15692 B. (116) Hedrich-Blessing 15692 C. (117) Hube Henry, Hedrich-Blessing 18809 L 5. (118) Bill Hedrich, Hedrich-Blessing 19715 S. (119) Hedrich-Blessing 19309 C. (120) Hedrich-Blessing 19715 V. (121) Hedrich-Blessing 21250 B. (122) Hedrich-Blessing 21250 A. (123) Hedrich-Blessing 21250 C. (124) Balthazar Korab. (125–128) The Office of Mies van der Rohe. (129) The Office of Mies van der Rohe. (130) Ezra Stoller © ESTO 41 T 4. (131) Ezra Stoller © ESTO 41 T 3. (132) Hedrich-Blessing 21451 E. (133) Hedrich-Blessing 21451 C. (134) Ezra Stoller © ESTO 41 T 32. (135) Ezra Stoller © ESTO 41 T 46. (136) Rollie McKenna 2/6. (137) Ezra Stoller © 41 T 9. (138) Ron Vickers Ltd 13572–12. (139) Ron Vickers Ltd 17092–1. (140) Ron Vickers Ltd 16756 M 18. (141) Ron Vickers Ltd 17092–3. (142) Panda/ Croydon Associates 67202–25. (143) The Office of Mies van der Rohe. (144) The Office of Mies van der Rohe. (145) The Office of Mies van der Rohe. (146) The Office of Mies van der Rohe. (147) The Office of Mies van der Rohe. (148) The Office of Mies van der Rohe. (149) Hedrich-Blessing 27043 S2. (150) Bill Engdahl, Hedrich-Blessing 27043 I. (151) Balthazar Korab 15853. (152) Hedrich-Blessing 27043 A2. (153) The Office of Mies van der Rohe. (154) The Office of Mies van der Rohe. (155) The Office of Mies van der Rohe. (156) Hedrich-Blessing 13686–E. (157) Hedrich-Blessing 22182 B. (158) Hedrich-Blessing 22182 D. (159) Hedrich-Blessing 9233 D. (160) Hedrich-Blessing 9969 E. (161) Hedrich-Blessing 9233 G. (162) Balthazar Korab 9622. (163) Balthazar Korab 9629. (164) Hedrich-Blessing 9969 C. (165) Hedrich Blessing 9969 A. (166) Hedrich-Blessing 13666 H. (167) Collection, The Museum of Modern Art, New York. Lens Craft 8810–1. (168) Hedrich-Blessing 13695. (169) Bill Engdahl, Hedrich-Blessing 17346 C. (170) Bill Engdahl, Hedrich-Blessing 17346 F. (171) Hedrich-Blessing 18837 P. (172) Hedrich-Blessing 18837 Q. (173) Hedrich-Blessing 16595. (174) Collection, The Museum of Modern Art, New York. 731.63. (175) The Office of Mies van der Rohe. (176) Hedrich-Blessing 33370 M2. (177) Hedrich-Blessing 33370 G2. (178) Hedrich-Blessing 33370 G3. (179) Hedrich-Blessing 33370 G3. (180) Hedrich-Blessing 33370 F3. (181) The

Office of Mies van der Rohe. (182) Hedrich-Blessing 33370 A.* (183) Bill Engdahl, Hedrich-Blessing 18506 Z2. (184) Hedrich-Blessing 16221. (185) Hedrich-Blessing 15412 A.* (186) Hedrich-Blessing 18809. (187) Hedrich-Blessing 10215 C. (188) Hedrich-Blessing 10216. (189) Bill Engdahl, Hedrich-Blessing 14490 T. (190) Hedrich-Blessing 14722. (191) Bill Hedrich, Hedrich-Blessing 15921 F. (192) Hedrich-Blessing 16329 H. (193) Suter, Hedrich-Blessing 21253 C. (194) Hedrich-Blessing 21308 B. (195) Reinhard Friedrich. (196) Hedrich-Blessing 27502 J. (197) Hedrich-Blessing 17378 E. (198) Hedrich-Blessing 19554 A. (199) Hedrich-Blessing 14490 T. (200) Hedrich-Blessing 18837 H. (201) Hedrich-Blessing 14722. (202) Werner Blaser. (203) Bill Hedrich, Hedrich-Blessing 14490 M. (204) Hedrich-Blessing 14490 T. (200) Hedrich-Blessing 18837 H. (201) Hedrich-Blessing 14722. Blessing 18837 J. (207) Hedrich-Blessing 18837 E. (208) Balthazar Korab 5329. (209) Hedrich-Blessing 18837 I. (210) Williams and Meyer Company 60–7670–2. (211) Hedrich-Blessing 16221. (212) Bill Engdahl, Hedrich-Blessing 18506 Q4. (213) Hedrich-Blessing 18837 D. (214) Hedrich-Blessing 18837–0. (215) Bill Engdahl, Hedrich-Blessing 18506 F4. (216) Bill Engdahl, Hedrich-Blessing 18506 U4. (217) Bill Engdahl, Hedrich-Blessing 18506 Q. (218) Balthazar Korab 5325. (219) Bill Hedrich, Hedrich-Blessing 15921 C. (220) Bill Hedrich, Hedrich-Blessing 15921 F. (221) Hedrich-Blessing 16329 D. (222) Hedrich-Blessing 16329 A. (223) Hedrich-Blessing 16329 B. (224) David Hirsch 498–23. (225) Hedrich-Blessing 27736 M. (226) Hedrich-Blessing 27502 J. (227) Phyllis Lambert. (228) Phyllis Lambert. (229) Phyllis Lambert. (230) Hedrich-Blessing 33370–02. (231) Hedrich-Blessing 33370–Q2. (232) Hickey & Robertson M–B195–6. (233) Hedrich-Blessing 33482 B. (234) Balthazar Korab 23. (235) Dirk Lohan 74471–3. (236) Bill Engdahl, Hedrich-Blessing 17378 D. (237) Hedrich-Blessing 17378 N. (238) Hedrich-Blessing 19554 A. (239) Williams & Meyer Company 80139. (240) Hedrich-Blessing 17378–0. (241) Hedrich-Blessing 17378 0. (242) Hedrich-Blessing 18766.* (243) Hedrich-Blessing 17378 G. (244) Hedrich-Blessing 17378 G. (245) Hedrich-Blessing 17378 G. (246) Hedrich-Blessing 17378 G. (247) Hedrich-Blessing 27736 J. (248) Hedrich-Blessing 17378 J. (249a, b, c) Hedrich-Blessing 17378 I. (250) Hedrich-Blessing 17378 L. (251) Hedrich-Blessing 17378 K. (252) Hedrich-Blessing 17356 B. (253) Hedrich-Blessing 17356 D. (254) Bill Engdahl, Hedrich-Blessing 17356 G. (255) Williams & Meyer Company 8000 1–1. (256) The Office of Mies van der Rohe. (257) The Office of Mies van der Rohe. (258) The Office of Mies van der Rohe. (259) The Office of Mies van der Rohe. (260) The Office of Mies van der Rohe. (261) Ron Vickers Ltd 16756 M35. (262) Ron Vickers Ltd 16756 .M34. (263) Ron Vickers Ltd 16756 M8A. (264) Panda/Croydon Associates 68854–27. (265) Werner Blaser. (266) Phyllis Lambert. (267) Hedrich-Blessing 72597. (268) Hedrich-Blessing 27358.* (269) Robert Pottinger 0572–5:5. (270) Hedrich-Blessing 33370 P. (271) Hedrich-Blessing 13666 D. (272) Werner Blaser. (273) Hedrich-Blessing 9767 A. (274) Hedrich-Blessing 19452 A. (275) Hedrich-Blessing 7890 B. (276) Hedrich-Blessing 13103 B. (277) Hedrich-Blessing 13809 S6.* (278) Bill Engdahl, Hedrich-Blessing 13809 I6. (279) Hedrich-Blessing 15489. (280) Bill Engdahl, Hedrich-Blessing 19153 D. (281) Hedrich-Blessing 19153 N.*

(282) Bill Engdahl, Hedrich-Blessing 19153 J. (283–285) Werner Blaser. (286) The Office of Mies van der Rohe. (287–288) Hedrich-Blessing 23315 C. (289) Hedrich-Blessing 28326 B. (290) Balthazar Korab 15075. (291) Hedrich-Blessing 23315 F. (292) Source unknown. (293) Hedrich-Blessing 21843. (294) Ezra Stoller © ESTO 41 T 8. (295) Hedrich-Blessing 21451 C. (296) Ezra Stoller © ESTO 41 T 5. (297) Werner Blaser. (298) Robert Wood. (299) Rollie McKenna II 3. (300) Robert Wood. (301) Balthazar Korab 15148. (302) Hedrich-Blessing 24366 E. (303) Bill Engdahl, Hedrich-Blessing 27043 F. (304) Hedrich-Blessing 22694 G. (305) The Office of Mies van der Rohe. (306) Hedrich-Blessing 27043 R2. (307) Balthazar Korab 15854. (308) Hedrich-Blessing 23513 L. (309) Hedrich-Blessing 23513 G. (310) Hedrich-Blessing 23513 B. (311) The Office of Mies van der Rohe. (312) Ron Vickers Ltd 16756 M 73. (313) The Office of Mies van der Rohe. (314) The Office of Mies van der Rohe. (315) Panda/Croydon Associates 68854–23. (316) Ron Vickers Ltd 13907–2. (317) Ron Vickers 16756 M 60. (318) Ron Vickers Ltd 16756 M 49. (319) Ron Vickers Ltd 16756 M 53. (320) Ron Vickers Ltd 16756 M 38. (321) Ron Vickers Ltd 16756 M 1. (322) Ron Vickers Ltd 16756 M 47. (323) Ron Vickers Ltd 16756 M 57. (324) Phyllis Lambert 119279–2. (325) Hedrich-Blessing 32833 G. (326) Hedrich-Blessing 32833 C. (327) Bill Hedrich, Hedrich-Blessing 32709 A2. (328) Hube Henry, Hedrich-Blessing 27770 E. (329) Hedrich-Blessing 32709 S. (330) Harr, Hedrich-Blessing 33637 A. (331) John Donat 1–8–68/108. (332) John Donat 1–8–68/105. (333) Hedrich-Blessing 31899 E. (334) Hedrich-Blessing 31899 F. (335) Hedrich-Blessing 31899 G. (336) Hedrich-Blessing 31899 H. (337) Hedrich-Blessing 31899 A. (338) John Donat 1–8–68 24/4. (339) Harr, Hedrich-Blessing 33637 C. (340) Ron Vickers Ltd 16756 M 66. (341) Peter Carter 126447–16. (342) Werner Blaser. (343) The Office of Mies van der Rohe. (344) Ron Vickers Ltd 16756 M 70. (345) Hube Henry, Hedrich-Blessing 26587 D. (346) Joseph J. Lucas, Jr. 3634. (347) Ezra Stoller © ESTO 41 T 18. (348) Balthazar Korab 5326. (349) Robert Pottinger. (350) Peter Carter. (351). Peter Carter. (352) Peter Carter 219697/20. (353) School of Architecture and City Planning, I.I.T. (354) School of Architecture and City Planning, I.I.T. (355) School of Architecture and City Planning, I.I.T. (356) School of Architecture and City Planning, I.I.T. (357) School of Architecture and City Planning, I.I.T. (358–363) School of Architecture and City Planning, I.I.T. All photographs by Richard Nickel. (364) School of Architecture and City Planning, I.I.T. (365) School of Architecture and City Planning, I.I.T. (366–376) School of Architecture and City Planning, I.I.T. All photographs except 370 are by Richard Nickel. (377) School of Architecture and City Planning, I.I.T. (378 and 379) School of Architecture and City Planning, I.I.T. (380) School of Architecture and City Planning, I.I.T. (381 and 382) School of Architecture and City Planning, I.I.T. (383 and 384) School of Architecture and City Planning, I.I.T. (385) School of Architecture and City Planning, I.I.T. (386) School of Architecture and City Planning, I.I.T. (387–390) School of Architecture and City Planning, I.I.T. (391) School of Architecture and City Planning, I.I.T. (392–397) School of Architecture and City Planning, I.I.T. (398 and JACKET) Bill Engdahl, Hedrich-Blessing 18506 K4. (399) Balthazar Korab 23. (400) The Office of Mies van der Rohe.

Index

Waynesburg College Library
Waynesburg, Pa.   15370